| Gangs

Other Books in the Current Controversies Series

Gangs

Noah Berlatsky, Book Editor

GREENHAVEN PRESS
A part of Gale, Cengage Learning

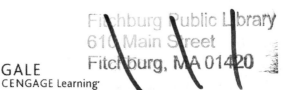

GALE
CENGAGE Learning·

Farmington Hills, Mich • San Francisco • New York • Waterville, Maine
Meriden, Conn • Mason, Ohio • Chicago

Patricia Coryell, *Vice President & Publisher, New Products & GVRL*
Douglas Dentino, *Manager, New Products*
Judy Galens, *Acquisitions Editor*

© 2015 Greenhaven Press, a part of Gale, Cengage Learning

WCN: 01-100-101

LIBRARY OF CONGRESS CATALOGING-IN-PUBLICATION DATA

Gangs / Noah Berlatsky, book editor.
    pages cm. -- (Current controversies)
    Includes bibliographical references and index.
    ISBN 978-0-7377-7217-3 (hardcover) -- ISBN 978-0-7377-7218-0 (pbk.)
    1. Gangs--United States. I. Berlatsky, Noah.
    HV6439.U5G35863 2015
    364.106'60973--dc23
                                                          2014024607

Printed in the United States of America
1 2 3 4 5 6 7 18 17 16 15 14

Contents

The majority of firearms in the hands of criminals in Chicago come from gun stores in the suburbs around the city. Criminals often get these guns through "straw purchases," which means that guns are bought legally by people with clean records and then resold. Regulating straw purchases is difficult in part because gun advocacy groups like the National Rifle Association have put pressure on the federal government not to investigate gun stores. However, there is evidence that investigations of gun stores and sting operations can lower the number of guns in the hands of criminals. More scrutiny of gun stores could therefore reduce gun and gang violence in Chicago.

In rural areas, which are often targeted as pro-gun and violence-ridden by liberals and the Barack Obama administration, gun deaths are quite low. The real problem with gun violence is in cities like Chicago and New Orleans. These areas have homicide rates as high as many failed states. Gun deaths are driven by gangs and criminal violence in urban areas not by gun ownership in the rest of America. The government needs to address gangs and rampant criminality rather than pushing for gun control.

Gang violence in the Caribbean often has very small-scale local causes. A wave of violence may be set off by one person with a gun going on a spree, resulting in waves of retaliation. Gang truces can be destabilizing and can lead to an increase in violence, rather than a reduction. Looking to larger causes—like drugs or poverty—may miss the small-scale immediate causes of gang violence, and may even provoke more shootings and deaths.

Gangs have deep historical roots in Latin American communities. They began as a form of communal self-protection and self-assertion and evolved, in the 1960s and 1970s, into advocacy groups seeking greater justice and civil rights for Latino people. However, the influx of drugs into inner-city neighborhoods during the 1980s pushed Latino gangs toward criminality and violence. The current approach to gangs involves repression and incarceration, which damages Latino communities further. Instead, antigang efforts should focus on youth contact and education to break the cycle of gangs and gang violence.

Social Media Has Led to an Increase in Gang Violence

Ben Austen

Young teens in Chicago's South Side neighborhoods often post videos online in which they threaten members of rival gangs. These boasts can escalate into real-life violence. The use of Facebook and the Internet to air public threats is a sign of how gangs in Chicago have changed. They are no longer centralized criminal enterprises but are mostly local cliques, without any hierarchical structure. The lack of central authority can result in more individual violence. But gang members' use of social media also gives police new tools, since they can sometimes follow disputes online and intervene before actual violence occurs.

Detroit Is Experiencing an Epidemic of Gang Violence

James A. Buccellato

Gang violence in Detroit is on the rise. In part, this is the result of past successful antigang activities, which broke up larger centralized corporate gangs. Gangs now in Detroit are neighborhood cliques, with no hierarchical structure; as a result, there is no organization to damp violence, and so there is more interpersonal violence, rather than less. In addition, urban poverty and the decay of Detroit civic institutions have left many young men in the city disconnected and desperate. Gang affiliation and gang violence is likely to persist as long as the problems of urban poverty and despair are not addressed.

Gang Violence Is Increasing in Denver

Sadie Gurman

Denver has instituted a program called Ceasefire, where gang members are gathered by police and civic leaders, warned of tough penalties if violence continues, and then given the opportunity to access social service programs to move away from gang violence. Ceasefire seems to have had little effect on gang violence, however, which is in fact rising rather than falling in the city. Police leaders say that the program will be effective in the long-term, but others express skepticism that the warnings are actually changing gang behavior.

New York has substantially decreased gun and gang violence since the early 1990s. This has been the result of proactive policing, where police intervene to stop and question—and sometimes stop and frisk—suspects who they believe might belong to gangs or be involved in gun violence. The press and Democratic candidates have criticized these stop-and-frisk tactics as unconstitutional and racist. However, the drop in New York's crime rate shows that these tactics are necessary, and that they especially benefit minority communities. Therefore, stop-and-frisk tactics should not be eliminated.

Chapter 3: Do Antigang Policies Violate Civil Rights?

Police gang units in the barrios of Denver, Colorado, and Ogden, Utah, constantly stop and harass Latino youth. Targeting gangs usually means targeting groups who fit gang descriptions, which means that any young men with tattoos, or wearing fashionable clothing, or just hanging out in a group may be stopped. The constant harassment suggests to the Latino communities that the police are working to control the population rather than to fight crime.

Inmates in California prisons can be confined to very restrictive, solitary confinement units called Security Housing Units (SHUs) if they are considered to be members of a gang. However, the evidence used to establish gang affiliation is often vague, including anonymous tips, having tattoos, or simply talking to someone who is thought to be in a gang. Those placed in SHUs have little hope of being released unless they inform against other gang members, which can leave them open to reprisals or be impossible if they are not in fact in a gang. California correctional facilities need to provide prisoners with due process, cease inhumane treatment, and scale back the use of SHUs.

No: Antigang Policies Do Not Violate Civil Rights

Accusations of police racial profiling in the Los Angeles Police Department (LAPD) are much exaggerated. Police use ethnicity as one criterion when looking at suspects of a certain description, but they do not stop or arrest people based on race. The accusations of racial profiling drive a wedge between police and the communities they serve. The LAPD should invest in video cameras for every police car, so that false accusations could be tested against the video and citizens could see that police are acting responsibly.

San Juan, Texas, police have established occasional checkpoints in specific areas where there have been criminal gang activities. At checkpoints people are questioned and, if they are in a gang, their photographs are taken for inclusion in a gang database. Civil liberties organizations are concerned that these searches are not constitutional. However, the police say that the searches are careful and targeted, that they help to reduce gang violence, and that they are not in violation of the US Constitution.

Chapter 4: What Is the Gang Problem Like in Other Countries?

The Economist

Mexico's government is struggling to deal with rampant gang murders, extortion, and kidnapping. The government of president Enrique Peña Nieto has poured resources into social services in the worst affected areas and is also trying to centralize security agencies and police. There has been some success in the reduction of murders, but kidnappings have actually risen. While the government claims its tactics are making progress against gangs, critics say they are ineffective and that the government is merely covering up the crime problem.

Jerry Langton

Violent targeted killings in Canada are linked to gang drug violence. Different Canadian gangs have links to the Italian mafia and to suppliers in Southeast Asia. Gang murders may involve disciplining of gang members who have become unreliable or violence between rival gangs. Either way, the violence in Canada is part of worldwide gang wars tied to the drug business.

Toby Muse

Columbia has supposedly had success in reducing violence by shutting down drug trafficking and drug gangs. However, much of the reduction in violence was due to the consolidation of the drug trade under one man, Diego Murillo. When Murillo was captured and imprisoned, violence in Medellín, Columbia, got worse rather than better, as rival gangs battled for control. Cocaine trafficking remains a serious problem, and young men turn to it as a way to make money and gain prestige. It is unlikely, therefore, that violence in Medellín will be curbed any time soon.

A new drug, spice, has become very popular in Russia. Concerns about the effects of the drug are rising, and street gangs have begun to attack some spice dealers. These gangs are technically illegal vigilantes, but they appear to be at least tacitly sanctioned by the Russian government, which has used gang violence before to police social unrest, demonstrations, and other threats to its rule.

Foreword

By definition, controversies are "discussions of questions in which opposing opinions clash" (*Webster's Twentieth Century Dictionary Unabridged*). Few would deny that controversies are a pervasive part of the human condition and exist on virtually every level of human enterprise. Controversies transpire between individuals and among groups, within nations and between nations. Controversies supply the grist necessary for progress by providing challenges and challengers to the status quo. They also create atmospheres where strife and warfare can flourish. A world without controversies would be a peaceful world; but it also would be, by and large, static and prosaic.

The Series' Purpose

The purpose of the Current Controversies series is to explore many of the social, political, and economic controversies dominating the national and international scenes today. Titles selected for inclusion in the series are highly focused and specific. For example, from the larger category of criminal justice, Current Controversies deals with specific topics such as police brutality, gun control, white collar crime, and others. The debates in Current Controversies also are presented in a useful, timeless fashion. Articles and book excerpts included in each title are selected if they contribute valuable, long-range ideas to the overall debate. And wherever possible, current information is enhanced with historical documents and other relevant materials. Thus, while individual titles are current in focus, every effort is made to ensure that they will not become quickly outdated. Books in the Current Controversies series will remain important resources for librarians, teachers, and students for many years.

In addition to keeping the titles focused and specific, great care is taken in the editorial format of each book in the series. Book introductions and chapter prefaces are offered to provide background material for readers. Chapters are organized around several key questions that are answered with diverse opinions representing all points on the political spectrum. Materials in each chapter include opinions in which authors clearly disagree as well as alternative opinions in which authors may agree on a broader issue but disagree on the possible solutions. In this way, the content of each volume in Current Controversies mirrors the mosaic of opinions encountered in society. Readers will quickly realize that there are many viable answers to these complex issues. By questioning each author's conclusions, students and casual readers can begin to develop the critical thinking skills so important to evaluating opinionated material.

Current Controversies is also ideal for controlled research. Each anthology in the series is composed of primary sources taken from a wide gamut of informational categories including periodicals, newspapers, books, US and foreign government documents, and the publications of private and public organizations. Readers will find factual support for reports, debates, and research papers covering all areas of important issues. In addition, an annotated table of contents, an index, a book and periodical bibliography, and a list of organizations to contact are included in each book to expedite further research.

Perhaps more than ever before in history, people are confronted with diverse and contradictory information. During the Persian Gulf War, for example, the public was not only treated to minute-to-minute coverage of the war, it was also inundated with critiques of the coverage and countless analyses of the factors motivating US involvement. Being able to sort through the plethora of opinions accompanying today's major issues, and to draw one's own conclusions, can be a complicated and frustrating struggle. It is the editors' hope that Current Controversies will help readers with this struggle.

Introduction

*"As [a 2011] FBI report suggests, the rise
in rural gangs is occurring in communities across the country."*

Gangs are generally thought of as a problem of cities or
urban areas. However, rural communities also have gangs
and gang violence. In fact, according to some reports, rural
gang activity has been rising noticeably in recent years. The
2011 National Gang Threat Assessment by the Federal Bureau
of Investigation (FBI) explained the threat as follows: "Gang
members are migrating from urban areas to suburban and rural communities to recruit new members, expand their drug
distribution territories, form new alliances, and collaborate
with rival gangs and criminal organizations for profit and influence."

As the FBI report suggests, the rise in rural gangs is occurring in communities across the country. A July 8, 2012, Associated Press report, for example, found that gang activity in
Tennessee cities with fewer than fifty thousand people had
more than tripled between 2005 and 2012. The report said
that gangs are moving into rural areas because of the promise
of new customers for drugs. In addition, rural areas "often
have small and sometimes ill-equipped police departments,"[1]
making it easier and safer for gangs to operate.

New Jersey also struggles with rural gangs. A 2010 police
report titled *Gangs in New Jersey* reported that the state had a
"widespread" gang presence, including in "urban, suburban,

---

1. Associated Press, "Gang Crime on Rise in Small Tennessee Cities," *TimesNews*,
July 8, 2012. http://www.timesnews.net/article/9048907/gang-crime-on-rise-in-small
-tennessee-cities.

and rural areas."[2] Lieutenant Edwin Torres, a special agent for the state Commission of Investigation's Organized Crime and Street Gang unit, said that there is a particular increase in school children joining gangs in rural New Jersey. Torres added that he had seen children as young as eight years old involved in gangs. "New Jersey has a significant gang problem that hits all counties,"[3] he explained, and said that rural parents need to be aware of the increasing dangers of gang activity in those parts of New Jersey.

Rural gangs are also a problem in the Pacific Northwest. In an August 4, 2011, report on National Public Radio, Austin Jenkins explains that police in the area are "grappling with gang rivalries, graffiti and even drive-by shootings."[4] Some of the violence occurs in small towns, but some of it is centered in public recreation areas, like parks and fishing holes. Jenkins writes that in Grant County in central Washington, there are four hundred gang members in a population of only eighty-five thousand people. In 2010, there were three gang-related homicides. Jenkins reports visiting a fishing spot where signs, public bathrooms, and rocks were all covered with graffiti in red and blue, the colors of the rival Norteno and Soreno gangs. Officer Chad McGary told Jenkins, "I have three kids myself and I don't come down here unless I'm armed and I know where I'm going to be fishing."[5] McGary said that gang members have even been known to target police officers. His own home was burglarized, and the culprits left a gang tag.

2. New Jersey Department of Law & Public Safety, *Gangs in New Jersey: Municipal Law Enforcement Response to the 2010 NJSP Gang Survey*, 2010. http://www.njsp.org/info/pdf/gangs_in_nj_2010.pdf.

3. Quoted in Meghan Shapiro Hodgin, "As More Gangs Move to Rural N.J., Expert Says Parents Need to Be Informed," nj.com, October 3, 2012. http://www.nj.com/somerset/index.ssf/2012/10/program_aims_to_help_parents_k.html.

4. Austin Jenkins, "Living in Gangland: Rural Gangs Claim Public Lands," NPR, August 4, 2011. http://www.npr.org/templates/story/story.php?storyId=135253412.

5. Ibid.

"They put a big SSL on there, Southside Crazy Boys, saying this is the gang that took your stuff," McGary said.

Gangs have also started to become active in rural areas on Native American reservations. The Pine Ridge Reservation in South Dakota, for example, has an 85 to 90 percent unemployment rate, with more than 90 percent of its residents living below the poverty line. Life expectancy is only forty-eight years for men and fifty-two for women, according to a November 23, 2012, article by Jay Scott Smith at *The Grio*.

Given these conditions, the appeal of money from illegal drug and gun sales is obvious. Representatives from Mexican drug cartels pay tribal members thousands of dollars to grow marijuana. The involvement in illegality can lead easily to violence. A member of the Native Mob in Minneapolis, a large Native American gang, was charged with shooting a witness in the presence of his five-year-old son. Smith writes that violence on the reservations still does not approach the level of cities like Chicago and Detroit, but it could worsen quickly if the issues of poverty and unemployment are not addressed.

Current Controversies: Gangs examines the issue of gangs in the United States, as well as in other countries, in such chapters as "What Causes Gangs and Gang Violence?," "Are Gangs and Gang Violence Increasing in the United States?," "Do Anti-gang Policies Violate Civil Rights?," and "What Is the Gang Problem Like in Other Countries?" Different commenters offer a range of perspectives on the roots and seriousness of gang violence and how to address it.

CHAPTER 1

What Causes Gangs and Gang Violence?

Chapter Preface

Marijuana has often been cited as a cause of gangs and gang violence. For example, in 2007, the White House Office of National Drug Control Policy (ONDCP) released a report suggesting that teens who used marijuana were "more likely to engage in violent and delinquent behavior."[1] Early marijuana use, the report said, was a predictor of gang activity later in life. The report prompted ONDCP director John Waters to declare, "Drug use by teenagers isn't a 'lifestyle choice' or an act of 'personal expression'; it is a public health, and, increasingly, a public safety dilemma."[2]

Marijuana is often economically central to gang and criminal activity. Tony Thompson in a September 2, 2010, article for the *London Evening Standard* reported on marijuana farms in Britain run by criminal gangs, often controlled by Vietnamese immigrants. Thompson noted that the illegal gang-controlled business can lead to violence, as in the murder of Khach Nguyen, who was beaten to death when the shipment of marijuana he was carrying was stolen and he could not pay the gang back. "It . . . seems certain that the violence associated with the trade is set to grow,"[3] Thompson concluded. Similarly, Jason Beaubien in a May 19, 2010, article at NPR pointed out that marijuana is "Mexico's biggest agricultural

---

1. Quoted in Phillip Smith, "ONDCP Kicks Off Annual Summer Marijuana Scare with Report Linking Drugs to Gangs, Violence," StoptheDrugWar.org, June 21, 2007. http://stopthedrugwar.org/chronicle/2007/jun/21/feature_ondcp_kicks_annual _summe.

2. Ibid.

3. Tony Thompson, "Untold Profits Fuel the Violent Gang World of London's Cannabis Farms," *London Evening Standard*, September 2, 2010. http://www.standard.co.uk /lifestyle/untold-profits-fuel-the-violent-gang-world-of-londons-cannabis-farms -6509328.html.

export," and that "[by] some estimates, it is the most profitable product for the Mexican drug gangs."[4]

Other commentators, though, argue that the violence associated with marijuana is not caused by the drug itself but is rather the result of its criminalization. A 2011 op-ed at the Marijuana Policy Project compares marijuana prohibition to alcohol prohibition and quotes the deputy police chief of Minneapolis, who said, "It is illegal to distribute marijuana, so the people distributing marijuana are criminal syndicates that are engaged in very violent activity to protect their turf."[5] The op-ed argues that the "only real solution to the prohibition-fueled violence is to regulate marijuana, and bring its sale under the rule of law, the same way we ended the criminal violence that stemmed from alcohol prohibition."

That conclusion is echoed by Andrea Woo in an October 27, 2011, article in the *National Post*. Woo quotes Dr. Evan Wood, an urban health researcher in British Columbia, as saying, "The gang warfare that's playing out on our streets is a natural consequence of cannabis prohibition."[6] Woo also pointed to polls showing that 50 percent of Canadians want to legalize marijuana. Marijuana advocate Jodie Emery cited the poll figures and argued, "It's a huge number of people who say their money is being wasted, police resources are being wasted and people's lives are being destroyed."[7]

The rest of this chapter will look at other factors often cited as causes of gangs and gang violence, such as the use of drugs other than marijuana, guns, racism, and poverty.

4. Jason Beaubien, "Cash from Marijuana Fuels Mexico's Drug War," NPR, May 19, 2010. http://www.npr.org/templates/story/story.php?storyId=126978142.

5. Quoted in Marijuana Policy Project, "It's Not the Marijuana but It's Prohibition That Fuels Crime," July 21, 2011. http://www.mpp.org/media/op-eds/its-not-the-marijuana-but.html.

6. Quoted in Andrea Woo, "Pot Prohibition Fuels Gang Violence in B.C.: Report," *National Post*, October 27, 2011. http://news.nationalpost.com/2011/10/27/pot-prohibition-fuels-gang-violence-report.

7. Ibid.

Gangs Form in Response to a Breakdown of Law and Order

Russell S. Sobel and Brian J. Osoba

Russell S. Sobel is a professor in the department of economics at West Virginia University. Brian J. Osoba is a professor in the department of economics at Central Connecticut State University.

In the early 1970s, fewer than 300 cities cited having problems with youth gangs. Since then, gangs have been identified in all 50 states, with over 2500 cities reporting problems by the late 1990s. Anecdotal evidence, along with casual empiricism, has led many people to hold a strong belief that youth gangs are a serious problem because areas with more gang activity also tend to have higher rates of violent crime committed by youths. Simply put, the commonly accepted wisdom is that gangs cause violence.

Crime Causes Gangs

In this paper, we propose and test a hypothesis suggesting that the causal relationship between youth violence and gang activity might flow in the exact opposite direction of what is commonly accepted. We propose that the failure of government to protect the rights of individuals from violence *committed by* youths has led to the formation of gangs as protective agencies among those populations who are most victimized by unpunished juvenile offenders in areas with high preexisting rates of violent crime. By banding together under the threat of mutual retaliation, potential victims of youth violence can secure increased safety. This same phenomenon also explains the widespread prevalence of gangs within prisons, where the rights of individuals are largely unenforced. While gangs, like governments, use coercion and violence to enforce their rules through retaliation, the net impact of gangs (like governments) is likely to lower the overall amount of violence. Generally, for an equilibrium to exist in which gang-type agencies prevail, the deterrence effect must reduce violence by more than the amount of violence used by the enforcement agency.

Government may actually increase the criminal effectiveness of gangs by using stricter enforcement measures.

Our analysis is solidly founded in the economic literature on the formation and evolution of "governments" from a situation of anarchy developed by [Robert] Nozick (1974) and [James M.] Buchanan (1975). These authors, particularly Nozick, explain how and why infant governments evolve as protection firms in the anarchistic "Hobbesian jungle,"[1] characterized by violence and theft. Assuming that protection firms already exist, [Daniel] Sutter (1995) uses a game-theoretic model to address the behavior of and relations between individual protection firms and their respective clients when there are varying levels of symmetry between the former and the latter. While other authors, such as [Oriana] Bandiera (2003), have previously applied this theoretical framework to the evolution of specific protection firms, like the Sicilian mafia, very little has been done on applying this model to youth gangs, with the exception of a purely theoretical model by [Stergios] Skaperdas and [Constantinos] Syropoulos (1995). Our analysis of youth gangs also relies on several recent theories developed in the literature on anarchy and whether it is welfare improving relative to a predatory state.

---

1. Thomas Hobbes was a philosopher who said human beings were inherently violent and that state control was needed to reduce violence.

Private Protective Agencies

In this paper, we develop this youth gang application of government evolution and anarchy theory to a much greater extent than has previously been done in the literature, and then conduct empirical testing. Our hypothesis—that gangs form in areas where there is a high rate of preexisting violence as a protection agency substituting for the lack of government enforcement of rights—is an alternative explanation for the well-documented cross-sectional correlation between gang activity and violent crime. In particular we show that our model predicts an exactly opposite direction of causality between youth gang activity and the rate of violent crime from what is commonly accepted. Because our hypothesis relies on the causality flowing from crime to gang membership rather than vice versa, we use empirical causality models to test our hypothesis. We indeed find a one-way causal relationship that violent crime causes gang membership, and we can reject the hypothesis that gang membership causes violent crime.

Our results have significant implications for government policy directed toward youth gangs. Just as the overthrowing or dissolving of a government in a geographic area might result in more violence because of a lack of rights enforcement in the resulting anarchy, government policy aimed at dissolving youth gangs will not be successful in reducing violent crime, and may in fact increase it. By failing to adequately punish youth offenders when they violate the rights of other individuals, the current government legal system has created an environment where there is a significant demand for these private protective agencies (youth gangs). While gangs do use violence to enforce their rules and protect the rights of their members, the net result of gangs, according to our results, is to reduce the amount of violent crime because of mutual deterrence. Because there will always be a market for private protection when government fails to protect individual rights, the implications are clear for how public policy reform can reduce gang activity: more effective enforcement of laws that protect the rights of individuals from violent crimes committed by youthful offenders. Breaking up and destabilizing gangs within our model is violence increasing, rather than violence reducing.

Our findings suggest policy implications that are sometimes contrary to the existing deterrence literature. The older theoretical literature on the deterrence effect indicates that stricter law enforcement is less effective than better detection. These models, however, deal with single offenders and not gangs. [Nuno] Garoupa (2007), on the other hand, actually addresses punishment as it relates to gangs. The author finds that government may actually increase the criminal effectiveness of gangs by using stricter enforcement measures. Also, Garoupa (2000) stipulates that government should impose less severe punishment on relatively nonviolent gangs because those gangs are likely more efficient in controlling criminal activity than is government. Government should instead focus its efforts on controlling violent gangs that use "costly extortion." The results of this paper suggest that Garoupa's (2000) solution is indeed the appropriate policy response to gang activity.

Within the economic model of protection services, an intervention that resulted in weakened gangs (or weakened governments) would result in more violence, not less.

This does not mean to say that all gang activity is explained by these differentials in enforcement. Sociological explanations and other factors surely play a major role. We also note that in some other countries with softer juvenile punishments, gangs are less prevalent. However, the fact that many gang members report joining a gang for protection, both among prison and youth gangs, suggests that the effect we examine is important nonetheless. What is important for deterring crime is whether the individual *committing* the crime is punished. When offenders go unpunished by the formal legal system, informal gangs help to fill this role, providing protection for those who would be potential victims of the unpunished offenders.

Drugs Do Not Explain Gangs

Sociologists and criminologists have weighed in most heavily on the debates regarding gang formation. [Irving] Spergel et al. (1996a) theorize that youth gang problems are brought about by several community-level factors, including a lack of both social opportunities and social organization, institutional racism, and failures of social policy. They claim that, especially in black neighborhoods, the street gang provides control and employment opportunities that are not provided by legally recognized institutions. The popular perception is that gangs, like the infamous Bloods and Crips, seek out new markets in which to franchise their names. However, the empirical literature has found results that reject this hypothesis. For example, Spergel et al. (1996b) note that most new gangs are not franchises. This is later reaffirmed by [Cheryl L.] Maxson (1998).

Other authors have hypothesized that gangs are little more than organized drug-dealing firms, and that the main reason for gang existence is the fact that drugs are illegal. This claim is widely made by law enforcement officials. While it is true that some gangs use the drug trade to help finance their activities, the empirical literature has uniformly provided results that reject the view that drug activity is the main reason for gang formation and existence. Maxson (1995) tests the connection between street gangs, illicit drug sales, and violence and finds that street gangs are far less likely to be involved in the illegal drug trade and the associated violence than the law enforcement literature suggests. The author finds that only a few gangs seemed to specialize in drug sales. [Steven D.] Levitt and [Sudhir A.] Venkatesh (2000) describe the inner workings of a gang that, in fact, does sell drugs. However, the gang charges an additional membership fee for those who wish to sell drugs.

One reason to be very skeptical of these claims by law enforcement officials of the gang relationship with the drug trade is because if law enforcement exaggerates the extent to which gangs are involved in drug trade, they are more likely to get bigger budgets. The fact that budgetary considerations play a major role in the decisions and actions of police departments is now widely demonstrated in the literature by authors such as [David W.] Rasmussen and [Bruce L.] Benson (1994).

Gangs as Protection

That gang activity is present to a greater extent in areas with higher rates of violent crime has been well demonstrated *in the cross section*. Based on this strong correlation, it is widely accepted that the way to reduce violent crime is to reduce gang activity. Inherent in this statement is an underlying assumption about the direction of causation between violent crime and gang activity. An intervention that reduces gang activity will only reduce violent crime if gangs cause violent crime. All protection firms and organizations, from the mafia to private security to traditional governments, use coercion, retaliatory violence, and predatory violence to enforce certain rules of conduct and to enforce and protect the rights of their members. However, saying that gangs cause violence based on this observed behavior is identical to claiming that governments that use coercion and violence as a means to provide protection services are causing more total violence than would exist without any government in place. The gang's use of retaliatory violence against someone who aggresses against a gang member actually results in a lower level of total violence as it creates a strong incentive for individuals not to initiate violence to begin with because of the fear of retaliation by the gang. Within the economic model of protection services, an intervention that resulted in weakened gangs (or weakened governments) would result in more violence, not less.

Our results provide strong evidence that violent crime causes an increase in gang membership, and not vice versa.

Any theory of gangs should be accepted or rejected based on its ability to explain real-world empirical observations. As we have already discussed, the real-world evidence rejects the hypothesis that gangs franchise and that they primarily form to participate in the drug trade (although it may be a secondary function performed by the gang once it is organized). Perhaps the most useful empirical observation that must be explained by a good theory of gang formation is why these gangs are primarily present among youths and not adults. The most widely accepted reason within law enforcement and in sociology is that gangs *employ* and recruit youth members because these members can commit crimes virtually without punishment because of their age. In this framework, youths are employed to coerce other individuals and commit violent acts to obtain resources for the gang leaders. Data on the age distribution of gang members, however, is notably inconsistent with this view. . . .

If gang members are employed based upon their ability to commit illegal acts without punishment from law enforcement, there should be a large, discrete decline in gang membership beginning at age 18. The age distribution of youth gang membership, however, does not show a significant drop at exactly age 18, but rather tapers off through the mid-twenties. This is a widely recognized puzzle in the standard theory.

Our hypothesis—that repeated violence committed by youths who then go unpunished causes gangs to subsequently form among the potential *victims* of this violence—does a better job of explaining the true age profile of gang membership. Because social groups and interactions do tend to be stratified by age, our theory also predicts that gangs would form among youths more than adults. However, within our model the age distribution of gang membership should begin to smoothly decline after age 18 as individuals move into new social groups as they age. The fact that both a 16-year-old and an 18-year-old are just as likely to be the victim of a 17-year-old criminal explains why our model fits this data better than the existing, and more commonly accepted, view of youth gangs. Both our later finding, that gangs lower net violence, and the fact that there is a gradual erosion of gang membership with age also provide some empirical support for the model by Sutter (1995). In that model, when exit is easier for members, the gang will tend to be more protective rather than predatory. . . .

A Failure of Government

The popular perception that gangs cause violent crime is based on tenuous casual observations. Although gangs and violence do seem to frequently coexist, such cross-sectional correlations do not imply causality. Our results provide strong evidence that violent crime causes an increase in gang membership, and not vice versa. Thus, areas with higher rates of violent crime will also experience higher rates of gang membership *as a result* of the increased violence.

We extend the models of government formation out of anarchy developed by Nozick (1974) and Buchanan (1975) and apply them to the relative anarchy faced by inner-city youths both at school and in their neighborhoods. Our analysis is based on the observation that government does not adequately protect the rights of individuals from violent crime committed by youths. Based on past violence or perceived future violence, these youths seek protection by forming organizations to provide safety where government public safety agencies have failed.

Our results are important because they uncover a situation where public policy, implemented with the best possible intentions, may in fact be harming those it was intended to help. As we have shown in all but one instance, violent crime leads to an increase in gang membership, not vice versa. If policies are enacted to break up gangs, the resulting increased anarchy should in fact lead to more violence among youths. This is because the gangs serve as a net deterrent of violence. In addition, as theorized by Buchanan (1973) and later by [Kai A.] Konrad (1999) and Skaperdas (2001), increased competition between gangs will lead to additional violence. Unless the already existing violence is mitigated, youths from the previous gangs will again form gangs. However, as these new gangs are smaller and more fragmented, more violence will occur.

Our main policy implication is that governments should try harder to protect the rights of individuals who are the victims of violence or coercion by juvenile offenders. Youths form and join gangs to secure protection primarily because of the inability or unwillingness of police and school administrators to protect their rights by punishing those juveniles who commit or threaten violence. When schools and inner cities are Hobbesian jungles, with little rights protection, it is only natural for individuals to seek protection in the private sector by forming gangs. While law enforcement likely is active in many of these city neighborhoods, the emphasis may be too heavily focused on prosecuting those participating in the illicit drug trade, in lieu of more directly protecting public safety and individual rights. These same implications apply to prison gangs in that they exist due to the lack of formal enforcement of the rights of inmates against aggression and violent acts committed by other inmates. Unless government improves on the protection it provides to individuals who are the potential victims of crimes, others will continue to join gangs to purchase these missing protective services currently underprovided by the government sector.

Gangs Are an Outgrowth of Poverty and Discrimination

Mikki Kendall

Mikki Kendall writes for The Guardian, The Toast, *and other publications, and is the cocreator of the website Hood Feminism.*

This is a love letter to the inner city. This is a love letter to a concept of Chicago that is constantly under attack. This is a love letter to the people in the hood who raised me, sustained me, and supported me.

Chicago Violence in Context

I've been trying to write about Chicago violence for a good two months now. The facts are easy to obtain from any major news source, though the way in which those facts are presented leaves a lot to be desired. Context matters, though, and it appears to be completely missing from most discussions concerning my city. If you were to take a map of Chicago marked with the neighborhoods with the highest rates of violence, and overlay it with a map of school closures, you might begin to see a pattern. Add in yet another map of cuts to public transit—including the decisions to shut down train lines for repairs for months or years at a time—and a picture emerges of neighborhoods that have been systematically isolated.

Experts on Chicago (who often are neither from Chicago or remotely educated about Chicago politics or Chicago history), often disparage the people in the community. And no, I'm not making excuses for gang violence. But when we talk about violence in the communities where gangs are most common, we have to talk about the economics of crime. We have to talk about the impact of poverty, of police brutality, of school closures, of services being cut over and over again to these neighborhoods. We have to talk about the impact of racism on wealth building in communities of color. We have to talk about politicians who think the solution to crime is to throw civil liberties out the window. We have to talk about why the institutional reaction to white-on-white violence was settlement houses, while the institutional reaction to violence in predominantly Black and Latino communities is to bring in the National Guard.

It's easy to forget that the people living in those neighborhoods are more complex than a sound bite, when those sound bites are often all that make it into the mainstream media. There's this idea that the community is responsible for fixing itself, as though these things are happening because the people living there have dozens of choices and they choose the ones that leads to violence.

> *Stop trying to fight fire with fire, and start fighting it with the water of access and opportunity. The violence is the symptom, but poverty is the disease.*

Race and PTSD

Discussions of mental health issues—like post-traumatic stress disorder—stop when race and crime enter the equation. Yet we know that kids who witness violence early in life are more likely to struggle with depression, anxiety, and yes, PTSD. We know that the kids who join gangs often come from unstable homes. Yet all too often, sympathy for the victims is as minimal as it is for the people doing the shooting. When you look at comments on articles about gun violence here, the racists usually come out to play. They're happy to lambast poor people of color for living in the only places they can afford in a rapidly gentrifying city where rents have more than tripled in the last 15 years. When discussions start about "those people," I am always aware that I am one of those people. I call it "hood made good" because—like a lot of the people I grew up with—I know what it's like to be poor in dangerous areas, and have to navigate the reality that the police aren't there to protect and serve you. To know that some of your neighbors are both a problem and a solution. Community policing is a joke in a city where calling the cops might get you help, or might get you killed.

That's before we get into the reality of poverty, and how often crime is all that's paying the most basic of bills in homes teetering on the edge of collapse. Survival demands certain hard choices, and while I have the privilege of not having to face those choices myself, I come from a family that faced them for me.

Chicago can be a hard city to love, especially in the depths of a violent summer. But make no mistake; the hood is not a cancer to be cut away. The hood needs healing and access to resources and opportunities that have vanished with each wave of gentrification. Want to stop the violence in Chicago? Save Chicago from a long slow decline into whatever post-apocalyptic wasteland is most popular in the imaginations of those who speak of sending armed troops into faltering neighborhoods? Stop trying to fight fire with fire, and start fighting it with the water of access and opportunity. The violence is the symptom, but poverty is the disease. Attack it with quality schools, health care for bodies and minds, jobs that pay living wages, public transit, open libraries, community centers, and policing strategies that don't involve brutality.

A Structural Problem

Instead of spending taxpayers' dollars to pad the wallets of wealthy institutions, polish up schools that are still brand new, spend that money in the hood. Commit to helping not just this generation, but the next several generations so "hood made good" is not the exception. I succeeded because of the sacrifices made on my behalf; I make sacrifices for my community; but this is not an individual problem. This is a structural problem that dates back generations. From the riots of 1919 [in which white ethnic groups attacked blacks] to the abuses of the '80s to the brutality of today, the hood in Chicago has been under attack longer than most of us have been alive. A people under siege cannot, will not be able to achieve their full potential. Chicago needs to write a love letter to itself.

Chicago Gangs Don't Have to Go Far to Buy Guns

Frank Main

Frank Main is a staff writer at the Chicago Sun-Times.

You might think the Deep South is the biggest source of the firearms in the hands of Chicago's criminals.

Chuck's Gun Store

Maybe you heard about the less-restrictive gun laws in the South or the high-profile cases the feds have brought against gun traffickers moving weapons from Mississippi and other states to Chicago—the Dixie pipeline.

But the truth is most guns recovered in crimes here were originally bought in Illinois.

More specifically, in Cook County [the county including Chicago].

And the No. 1 supplier of those weapons is just a short drive from Chicago, Chuck's Gun Store in south suburban Riverdale.

From 2008 to March 2012, the police successfully traced the ownership of 1,375 guns recovered in crimes in Chicago within a year of their purchase.

Of those guns, 268 were bought at Chuck's—nearly one in five.

That statistic comes from a groundbreaking study by University of Chicago Crime Lab researchers, done at the request of the Chicago Police Department, which is grappling with an extra-violent 2012 that has seen a 28 percent spike in the city's homicide total compared to this time last year.

In their study, U. of C. researchers combed through gun-trace data to determine the weapons most likely bought by straw purchasers.

Those are people without criminal records who buy guns for felons—often at a hefty markup.

Fifty-eight percent of those recovered guns were bought in Illinois. About 19 percent were purchased in Indiana, 3 percent in Wisconsin—and less than 2 percent in Mississippi.

Cook County was the source of 45 percent of the guns over that period, according to the crime lab's study.

Roseanna Ander, executive director of the lab, said the new findings suggest a key strategy to keeping guns off the street is for law-enforcement agencies to target the local gun stores most likely to sell firearms to straw purchasers.

But the laws on the books make it tough for prosecutions against shady gun dealers who follow the letter but not the spirit of the law.

And that's against a backdrop of a well-funded gun lobby and an underfunded federal enforcement effort—a combination that undermines crackdowns on gun dealers.

Straw purchasing cases are rare compared to cases involving illegal gun possession and other types of firearm offenses.

Cases Against Shop Owners Rare

Police conducted stings on suburban gun stores in the late 1990s, but those investigations produced mixed results and they haven't been done consistently for years.

"Firearms dealers are so well protected it makes it really hard to prosecute them. It has to be very, very egregious," said

Mark Jones, a retired supervisor for the U.S. Bureau of Alcohol, Tobacco, Firearms and Explosives.

Still, "having the dealers know people are paying attention again and are willing to act could have an impact," Ander said.

In recent years, some people have been convicted of making straw buys at Chuck's and other stores in the area.

But straw purchasing cases are rare compared to cases involving illegal gun possession and other types of firearm offenses.

Rarer still are convictions of the owners of gun stores.

In 2009, Ugur Yildiz, owner of Chicagoland Bells in Franklin Park, was sent to prison for more than seven years for illegally exporting arms to Canada. And in 2002, two former owners of an Elmwood Park gun shop were sentenced to probation for falsely identifying the buyer of two pistols on federal forms.

Those are the exceptions.

Most of the suburban store owners who were the subjects of stings in the late '90s were acquitted of gun charges.

John Riggio, owner of Chuck's, has never been charged with wrongdoing involving his store.

The shop is small-town charming, its walls adorned with Bears and Sox posters and a photo of the Lone Ranger.[1] There's also a sign warning customers it's illegal to buy guns and ammo for someone else.

Riggio declined to talk on the record, but privately he's happy to chat about the steps he takes to ensure he and his customers are following the law.

As he talked one recent day, a Dolton police officer walked into the store to say hello and helped a customer with questions about how he could legally transport his newly purchased gun in his car.

---

1. The Chicago Bears are a football team. The Chicago White Sox are a baseball team. The Lone Ranger is a fictional western vigilante.

Riggio and his store don't project the image of an arms dealer indifferent to whether guns wind up in the hands of criminals or honest citizens.

Still, he's been blasted over the years, accused of being an irresponsible gun dealer. The criticism began after a study showed Chuck's sold more guns between 1996 and 2000 that ended up in the hands of criminals than any store in the country.

The store is periodically targeted for protests by gun-control activists such as the Rev. Michael Pfleger and the Rev. Jesse Jackson. In one rally outside the store in 2007, Jackson yelled to hundreds of protesters: "Futures not funerals! Sons not guns!"

Often Stolen from Legitimate Buyers

Larry Pelcher, owner of Pelcher's Gun Shop and Shooters Supply Inc. in south suburban Lansing, didn't want to speak for Chuck's, but said he doubts any local gun stores are breaking the law.

The guns traced back to suburban Cook County stores have often been stolen from legitimate buyers who got them for protection.

And he doesn't think straw purchasers are the key reason guns are getting into criminals' hands in Chicago.

Store owners "go out of our way to ensure the person buying the firearm is legitimate and is not a straw buyer," Pelcher said.

The guns traced back to suburban Cook County stores have often been stolen from legitimate buyers who got them for protection, he said.

Police acknowledge stolen guns form part of the supply line to crooks.

In an interview with the *Chicago Sun-Times*, a South Side gang member admitted he and his crew almost exclusively arm themselves with stolen guns because they can't afford to buy new ones. Some of those guns, he said, are stolen from freight trains sitting in South Side rail yards. Others are swiped from gun stores.

To better track stolen weapons, Chicago Police Supt. Garry McCarthy is pushing for a law requiring gun owners to file a police report when their firearms are stolen, lost or transferred to another owner.

But stolen guns are only part of the supply.

The gang member interviewed by the *Sun-Times* also said weapons from straw purchasers are common, too. It's just another way to make money on the street.

Wealthy drug dealers in his South Side neighborhood buy those weapons from straw purchasers—usually for $100 or more above the retail price.

"The Charade"

The stream of guns from straw purchases continues because some gun dealers are engaged in a "charade" with crooked buyers, according to the former ATF agent, Jones, who worked for the bureau in Chicago and whose last assignment was as regional firearms adviser for Central America.

Most federally licensed gun dealers are smart enough to follow the letter of the law that bars them from selling to straw buyers.

So they check whether a customer has a valid Illinois firearm owner's identification card needed to buy a gun.

They conduct a background check to make sure the buyer isn't a crook.

But when they suspect a customer is a straw purchaser, some gun dealers don't follow the spirit of the law, Jones said.

They sell the gun anyway.

A shady deal might play out like this, Jones said:

Two men walk into a store. One has an Illinois FOID [Firearm Owners Identification] card needed to buy a gun. The other has only a driver's license.

The dealer tells the FOID cardholder: "I can't sell you a firearm unless you come in alone."

So a week later, the suspected straw purchaser returns, alone, and buys the gun his buddy wanted—but couldn't buy legally.

"It's a charade," Jones said. "It's very hard to prove a dealer 'knowingly and willfully' sold a gun to a straw purchaser."

But Pelcher, the gun store owner, said he and other store owners police themselves. He said they regularly circulate faxes among each other about suspicious shoppers they turn away.

[Chicago] now requires gun owners to obtain a permit through the Chicago Police Department and register their guns with the city.

On July 30, for instance, he got a fax that two men—one with an Illinois FOID card and one with a driver's license—walked into another store to look at guns. The storeowner told the men to leave. The fax included photos of the rejected buyers and warned: "These men attempted a straw purchase. They may try again elsewhere."

Pelcher insists he doesn't just follow the letter of the law. He goes beyond what the law requires, he says.

For instance, Pelcher says he tries to makes sure customers comply with Chicago's new gun registration requirements.

In 2010, the City Council passed a gun registration law after the U.S. Supreme Court declared the city's handgun ban unconstitutional. The city now requires gun owners to obtain a permit through the Chicago Police Department and register their guns with the city.

Pelcher said he checks potential customers' IDs to see whether they have a Chicago address. If they do, but they haven't received a Chicago gun permit, he'll ask where they plan to keep the gun.

Gun dealers are not required by law to bar people with Chicago addresses from buying firearms.

"If they present a valid FOID card but say they want one for protection in Chicago, I won't sell it to them, unless they're willing to have me hold the pistol until they get a Chicago permit," Pelcher said.

"We have been here long enough to know who they are when they walk into the store," he said. "When you have a woman walk into the store with a firearms card and you ask her a simple question about a gun and she doesn't know the answer, you know it's not for her. We'll turn her away."

But Jones said nailing such people for trafficking guns isn't easy.

He explained that store owners are required to report multiple handgun purchases by an individual. ATF officials can examine those records to flag potential straw purchasers, he said.

Yet, ATF is too short-staffed to do a proper job inspecting the records of the gun dealers, which the agency calls FFLs or federal firearms licensees, Jones said. He estimated that the average gun dealer is inspected every few years.

ATF also has an "investigative history of being extremely careful about how FFLs are handled," Jones said.

Falling Gun Prosecutions

The National Rifle Association and its allies in Congress have intensified pressure on the ATF, Jones said, to avoid conducting criminal investigations of gun dealers since the controversial "Fast and Furious" investigation, in which the agency failed to track straw-purchased weapons that wound up in Mexican drug cartel members' hands and were used to kill a U.S. Border Patrol agent.

Asked for statistics on how many gun cases ATF has submitted to prosecutors in recent years, a local spokesman for the agency referred the *Sun-Times* to a Syracuse University system that tracks federal prosecutions.

It showed the ATF office for the Northern District of Illinois had a decline in weapons prosecutions from fiscal year 2010 to 2011, and the trend was expected to continue the following year.

The U.S. attorney's office is no longer prosecuting most locally based gun cases involving straw purchasing.

Nationally, there's been "a shifting emphasis toward drug-related investigations," according to the analysis.

Over the past five years, meanwhile, prosecutors have shifted their strategy involving gun cases, according to records and interviews.

The U.S. attorney's office is no longer prosecuting most locally based gun cases involving straw purchasing. Instead, federal prosecutors have been focusing on interstate gun-trafficking rings and on felons who have guns illegally.

In recent years, federal and Cook County prosecutors have been meeting regularly to decide who will handle what gun cases in an effort to maximize potential sentences.

They realize straw buyers typically receive probation in the federal system because the defendants don't have criminal records.

So those cases are going to Cook County prosecutors who can seek stiffer sentences.

Federal prosecutors have won long prison terms for people convicted of illegal gun possession and out-of-state gun trafficking, according to a sampling of dozens of recent sentences.

On average, those defendants were being sent to federal prison for 10-year terms with only one sentence of probation.

A small sampling of straw purchasing cases prosecuted in Cook County also showed defendants' hefty sentences: four years on average.

But if you look at all gun-related Cook County sentences, the numbers tell a different story.

A *Sun-Times* study of gun-related sentences in the Cook County Criminal Courts showed judges favoring probation over prison sentences in most of the cases.

Most involved charges of unlawful use of a weapon—someone having a gun when they shouldn't—and not straw purchasing.

Based on thousands of criminal records obtained through a Freedom of Information request, the newspaper looked at gun cases that didn't involve other crimes.

Of more than 8,000 people sentenced between 2005 and March 2012, about 54 percent received probation and the others received prison or jail terms, the *Sun-Times* found.

"There is no certainty of consequences in Cook County for getting caught with a gun," said Nicholas Roti, chief of the Chicago Police Department's Bureau of Organized Crime.

To make sure gang-bangers get locked up, prosecutors have been using a new law enforcement weapon—the Valadez Law, named for slain Chicago Police Officer Alejandro Valadez. One of the three men charged in Valadez's June 2009 murder was on probation for aggravated unlawful use of a weapon, a gun possession charge.

The 2010 Valadez Law requires prison time for street gang members convicted of possessing a loaded gun in a public area.

New Ballistics Lab

To improve their ability to make gun cases, the Chicago Police are building a new ballistics laboratory because they say the State Police crime lab was taking too long to test recovered guns for evidence.

Authorities also are considering a new Cook County gun court dedicated to handling only firearms cases.

As for straw purchasers, some experts have called for legislators to require gun stores to install security cameras and allow authorities to review videotapes of those purchases. They also have suggested a ban on cellphones in gun stores to stymie straw buyers from taking orders from their customers.

Ander, the head of the University of Chicago Crime Lab, said undercover stings on gun stores also seem to have reduced the flow of crime guns from those locations—at least temporarily.

She pointed to a 2006 study by Johns Hopkins professor Daniel W. Webster that found stings were associated with an abrupt, year-long decline in the flow of new guns to criminals in Chicago.

"The scrutiny seemed to change their behavior," Ander said of the suburban gun stores after the stings of the late '90s.

"Given the magnitude of gun violence in Chicago, we should be employing all the tools in the toolbox that can make a dent in this problem."

Availability of Guns Does Not Fuel Gang Violence in Chicago

Daniel Greenfield

Daniel Greenfield, a Shillman Journalism Fellow at the Freedom Center, is a New York writer focusing on radical Islam. He is completing a book on the international challenges America faces in the twenty-first century.

Chicago's murder numbers have hit that magic 500. Baltimore's murder toll has passed 200. In Philly, it's up to 324, the highest since 2007. In Detroit, it's approaching 400, another record. In New Orleans, it's almost at 200. New York City is down to 414 from 508. In Los Angeles, it's over 500. In St. Louis it's 113 and 130 in Oakland. It's 121 in Memphis and 76 in Birmingham.

America's Gun Culture

Washington, D.C., home of the boys and girls who can solve it all, is nearing its own big 100.

Those 12 cities alone account for nearly 3,200 dead and nearly a quarter of all murders in the United States. And we haven't even visited sunny Atlanta or chilly Cleveland.

These cities are the heartland of America's real gun culture. It isn't the bitter gun-and-bible clingers in McCain and Romney[1] territory who are racking up a more horrifying annual kill rate than [terrorist organization] Al Qaeda; it's Obama's own voting base.

---

1. John McCain was the 2008 Republican presidential nominee; Mitt Romney was the 2012 Republican presidential nominee.

Chicago, where [President Barack] Obama delivered his victory speech, has homicide numbers that match all of Japan and are higher than Spain, Poland and pre-war Syria. If Chicago gets any worse, it will find itself passing the number of murders for the entire country of Canada.

Chicago's murder rate of 15.65 per 100,000 people looks nothing like the American 4.2 rate, the Midwestern 4.5 or the Illinois' 5.6 rates, but it does look like the murder rates in failed countries like Rwanda, Sierra Leone and Zimbabwe. To achieve Chicago's murder rate, African countries usually have to experience a bloody genocidal civil war or decades of tyranny.

But Chicago isn't even all that unique. Or the worst case scenario. That would be New Orleans which at an incredible 72.8 murder rate is ten times higher than the national average. If New Orleans were a country, it would have the 2nd highest murder rate in the world, beating out El Salvador.

Louisiana went red for Romney 59 to 40, but Orleans Parish went blue for Obama 80 to 17.

Any serious conversation about gun violence and gun culture has to begin at home; in Chicago, in Baltimore, in New York City, in Los Angeles and in Washington, D.C.

St. Louis has a murder rate just a little lower than Belize. Baltimore has a worse murder rate than South Africa and Detroit has a worse murder rate than Colombia. Obama won both St. Louis and Baltimore by comfortable margins. He won Detroit's Wayne County 73 to 26.

Guns, Obama Voters, and Gangs

Homicide rates like these show that something is broken, but it isn't broken among the Romney voters rushing to stock up on assault rifles every time Obama begins threatening their right to buy them; it's broken among Obama's base

Any serious conversation about gun violence and gun culture has to begin at home; in Chicago, in Baltimore, in New York City, in Los Angeles and in Washington, D.C.

Voting for Obama does not make people innately homicidal. Just look at Seattle which is agonizing over its 26 murders. That's about the same number of murders as East St. Louis which has only 27,000 people to Seattle's 620,000.

So what is happening in Chicago to drive it to the gates of hell ahead of Zimbabwe and Rwanda?

A breakdown of the Chicago killing fields shows that 83% of those murdered in Chicago last year had criminal records. In Philly, it's 75%. In Milwaukee it's 77% percent. In New Orleans, it's 64%. In Baltimore, it's 91%. Many were felons who had served time. And as many as 80% of the homicides were gang related.

Chicago's problem isn't guns; it's gangs. Gun control efforts in Chicago or any other major city are doomed because gangs represent organized crime networks which stretch down to Mexico, and trying to cut off their gun supply will be as effective as trying to cut off their drug supply.

America's murder rate isn't the work of the suburban and rural homeowners who shop for guns at sporting goods stores and at gun shows, and whom news shows profile after every shooting, but by the gangs embedded in the urban areas controlled by the Democratic machine. The gangs who drive up America's murder rate look nothing like the occasional mentally ill suburban white kid who goes off his medication and decides to shoot up a school. [Connecticut elementary school shooter Adam] Lanza, like most serial killers, is a media aberration, not the norm.

National murder statistics show that blacks are far more likely to be killers than whites and they are also far more likely to be killed. The single largest cause of homicides is the argument. 4th on the list is juvenile gang activity with 676 murders, which combined with various flavors of gangland killings takes us nearly to the 1,000 mark. America has more gangland murders than Sierra Leone, Eritrea and Puerto Rico have murders.

Our national murder rate is not some incomprehensible mystery that can only be attributed to the inanimate tools, the steel, brass and wood that do the work. It is largely the work of adult males from age 18 to 39 with criminal records killing other males of that same age and criminal past.

There is a war going on in America between gangs of young men who bear an uncanny resemblance to their courterparts in Sierra Leone or El Salvador.

If this were going on in Rwanda, El Salvador or Sierra Leone, we would have no trouble knowing what to make of it, and silly pearl-clutching nonsense about gun control would never even come up. But this is Chicago, it's Baltimore, it's Philly and NOLA [New Orleans, Louisiana]; and so we refuse to see that our major cities are in the same boat as some of the worst trouble spots in the world.

Lanza and Newtown [the site of Lanza's violence] are comforting aberrations. They allow us to take refuge in the fantasy that homicides in America are the work of the occasional serial killer practicing his dark art in one of those perfect small towns that always show up in murder mysteries or Stephen King [horror] novels. They fool us into thinking that there is something American about our murder rate that can be traced to hunting season, patriotism and bad mothers.

But go to Chicago or Baltimore. Go where the killings really happen and the illusion comes apart.

Gang Wars

There is a war going on in America between gangs of young men who bear an uncanny resemblance to their courterparts in Sierra Leone or El Salvador. They live like them, they fight for control of the streets like them and they kill like them.

America's horrific murder rate is a result of the transformation of major American cities into Sierra Leone, Somalia, Rwanda and El Salvador. Our murder rate now largely consists of criminals killing criminals.

As David Kennedy, the head of the Center for Crime Prevention and Control, put it, "The majority of homicide victims have extensive criminal histories. This is simply the way that the world of criminal homicide works. It's a fact."

America is, on a county by county basis, not a violent country, just as it, on a county by county basis, did not vote for Obama. It is being dragged down by broken cities full of broken families whose mayors would like to trash the Bill of Rights for the entire country in the vain hope that national gun control will save their cities, even though gun control is likely to be as much help to Chicago or New Orleans as the War on Drugs.

Obama's pretense that there needs to be a national conversation about rural American gun owners is a dishonest and cynical ploy that distracts attention from the real problem that he and politicians like him have sat on for generations.

We do not need to have a conversation about the NRA. We need to have a conversation about Chicago.

Gang Violence Can Have Small-Scale Local Causes

Sarah Stankorb

Sarah Stankorb is a contributing writer for CNNMoney *and* GOOD. *Her articles and essays have appeared in such publications as* The New York Times, The Atlantic, Salon, Kiwi, Babble, Geez, *and* The Morning News.

Imagine living in a neighborhood with 53 gang-related homicides in a single year—none solved. Eighty-six percent of your neighbors report having heard gunshots in the past month, but police are little help. Though few even bother to report crimes anymore because of fear of retaliation, when the police are called, more than three-quarters of the time, they don't show up in a timely manner.

The Caribbean Gangland

This is a statistical window into what it is like to grow up in a Caribbean gangland.

At a February 17 event that drew a crowd of diplomats, policy makers, U.S. and Caribbean researchers, AU's School of Public Affairs hosted the Inter-University Consortium for Caribbean Gang Research in a dialogue about the causes and potential responses to rampant gang crime and violence throughout much of the Caribbean.

Anthony Harriott, University of the West Indies–Mona Campus, gave a first-hand account of the situation in Jamaica. Though in much of the Caribbean, crime rates were traditionally relatively low (lower than some parts of Europe and the United States), a skyrocket in rates of violence over the last decade can be tightly correlated with gangs and organized crime. Less cohesive, less organized, often urban poor communities fall first to the control of gangs. They can become part of a broader system of corruption, where gangs keep people from the voting booth through intimidation in some communities and deliver votes to particular parties in others, thus securing control over neighbors and strong ties to those in political power.

Violent Crime Hotspots

The trouble is the difference between perception and fact. People living in communities with high poverty and failing police presence often come to rely upon local gang leaders, even though much of the violence they seek to mitigate by gang law is caused by the gangs themselves.

Among other presenters, Charles Katz, Arizona State University, and SPA professor Edward Maguire shared key findings from the pair's six-year research project in Trinidad. Their research challenges much of the accepted rhetoric surrounding gangs and how to shut them down.

The broader question of dismantling gangs—one which many policy makers have long focused upon—seems one or even ten steps past a logical starting point.

Maguire and Katz studied 10 gangs in four Trinidadian neighborhoods that were hotspots for violent crime, areas no broader than 600 feet long (or about a city block). In looking at violence specific to these neighborhoods, the researchers found rationales for violence greatly varied, indicating that theories of "root causes" of gang violence (i.e., poverty or the drug trade) were not acknowledged motivations for violence by these gang members.

In direct interviews with gang leaders, violence often was shown to have very local causes. In Trinidad, gang members killed people over perceived disrespect, territory, disputes over money or girls. They killed in retaliation, as part of internal power struggles, or in revenge for ratting to police.

According to Maguire, esoteric factors contribute to upticks in violence. "You've got one guy who just got out of prison and he's really angry, and he's got a gun, and he's got a set of people he wants to kill. There's not a 'root cause' there." In analysis, one could look deeper and possibly connect this one man's situation with broader cultural factors, but what is really instigating violence is a more proximate cause—an angry man with a gun.

Moreover, stop-the-violence efforts, including truces, have proved fatal in the long term. American research in Los Angeles and Chicago, though limited, showed that truces have not worked domestically. In Morvant, Trinidad, a truce resulted in a short-term drop in violence with a substantial increase in violence over time. Not all gangs agreed to participate in the truce. Some of those participating in the truce were perceived as weaker and became victims of crime, eventually spurring cycles of retaliation. Maguire gives an example from a gang, where "one gang leader was really angry that because of the truce, the police were no longer concentrating their efforts on the gangs participating in the truce and so now they were focusing their efforts on him, and that made him want to kill all of them."

In this context, the broader question of dismantling gangs—one which many policy makers have long focused upon—seems one or even ten steps past a logical starting point. As Maguire added at the end of his talk, "the bigger question is, how do we get gangs to stop shooting each other and shooting other people? How do we stop the violence?"

The stakes are clear. "Diagnosis is an essential part of solving any problem, including violence problems, and understanding these concentrations of violence is an essential step in that diagnostic process. It helps us understand potential solutions," explained Maguire. Assuming the roots of gang violence originate with causes like the drug trade, "cause us to put in place solutions that don't work ... sometimes they cause us to put in place solutions that make the problem worse."

Gangs Have Deep Roots in Latino Communities

Jimmy Franco Sr.

Jimmy Franco Sr. is the moderator and writer of the blog site Latino Point of View.

The recent focus on the issue of immigration reform and the media attention being given to Latinos have centered mostly upon the quantitative progress that has been made by this segment of society. These forward steps include an uptick in media roles, increased political involvement and attention from politicians, reports of higher rates of high school and college graduates and a growing cultural presence. However, the negative aspect that is developing, but which is not being discussed publicly by Latino leaders and politicians is the continuing growth of gangs, drug addiction, violence and incarceration that is occurring within our communities. This problematic element of gangs and their socially corrosive effect upon our youth and their families needs to be directly addressed and not ignored by hiding our heads in the sand in regard to this issue. Most people perceive this as primarily an inner-city problem and that if they move to the suburbs they can escape the violence and drugs associated with gangs. Yet, the phenomenal and continuing growth of gangs has also occurred within the suburbs and even small towns. This summer, in what is called "the killing season" in Los Angeles, there has been an increase in gang killings within the city and in its adjoining suburbs of Pomona and Compton. Many small towns such as Oxnard and others within the rural San Joaquin Valley like Salinas and Visalia are experiencing a growth in

Jimmy Franco Sr., "The Continuing Lure of Youth Gangs: Those Left Behind," *Latino Point of View* (blog), September 5, 2013. www.latinopov.com. Copyright © 2013 Jimmy Franco Sr. All rights reserved. Reproduced by permission.

gang involvement by Mexican-American youths. All of this wasteful and destructive activity has resulted in an increasing rate of imprisonment for many of these teenagers and adults. Mexican-Americans and other Latinos cannot fully progress while such a growing segment of our young people are losing their potential and future to drug and alcohol abuse, violence, and being locked up. The unwillingness to fully discuss and politically address this widening social problem by Latino political leaders and organizations is similar to a family that ignores and refuses to confront the negative and deepening behavioral problem of a particular family member by hoping that it will simply go away.

The increasing demand for drugs within our present society has spawned the growth of thousands of minority youth and adult gangs.

Youth Gangs Have a Long and Deep-Rooted Tradition in America

There have been gangs in this country ever since the early 1800's with membership comprised of various ethnic groups ranging from Irish, Italian, Jewish and others. The underlying factors that led to the formation of these early immigrant and first generation youth gangs were poverty, discrimination and a lack of education and opportunity. The first major gangs in Los Angeles were Irish and by the 1880's L.A. had become one of the most violent cities in the country due to the illegal activities of these newly formed gangs. These were later followed by Italian gangs who prospered during prohibition as bootleggers in the illegal liquor trade and who waged violence against their competitors to maintain dominance. In Los Angeles, the first Chicano gangs began to evolve during the 1920's and 1930's as a form of organization for self-defense from police violence and racial attacks and as a method of self-help and brotherhood against the barriers of segregation, racism and limited opportunities. Being from a certain barrio meant being proud of one's family and neighborhood and of the people living there as it was a haven that was to be defended from hostile intruders and an antagonistic society. Other factors contributed to the development of these fledgling Chicano youth gangs such as the need for an identity, pride and the camaraderie of group unity as the actual barrio and the neighborhood gang soon became intertwined over time. Some of the oldest barrios in Los Angeles such as 38th Street, Macy, Clanton 14, Palo Verde and EastSide Clover began over 80 years ago within the inner-city while others also developed at this time within the Maravilla section of East L.A. and in many long-established barrios such as San Fernando, Pico-Rivera and San Gabriel. The outbreak of the 1943 Zoot Suit riots in Los Angeles witnessed a united front of Chicano gangs who fought back and defended their neighborhoods against the racial assaults of rampaging white mobs made up of rioting Marines and sailors. However, the ongoing negative factors associated with gang life such as ethnic self-hatred, low self-esteem, violence, excessive drug and alcohol use and a scorn for education have resulted in generations of countless lives being harmed and destroyed. Up until the late 1970's many fights among gangs primarily involved the use of fists and knives as the widespread use of guns was rare while the low-level sale and use of drugs were mostly for personal use in contrast to today's large-scale and profitable drug businesses.

The 1970's Chicano Civil Rights Movement and the Role of Gangs

The progressive nationalism that occurred during the 1970's contributed to the growth of a strong sense of identity and pride along with a yearning for unity and civil rights among young Mexican-Americans. This political movement also affected many youthful gang members in addition to those who were locked up within the prisons. In Los Angeles, many ex-gang members who had acquired a sense of political consciousness changed their lives and joined youth groups such as the Brown Berets, La Junta and the college MEChAs in order to work together to improve their communities. The series of National Chicano Moratorium protest marches against the Vietnam War that were held in East Los Angeles resulted in the formation of a broad coalition of gangs which discouraged barrio violence and other destructive acts within their neighborhoods. This gang coalition joined the growing political movement for civil rights and helped to drastically decrease gang violence and other destructive acts within their communities by establishing a truce and promoting unity among these youthful groups. African-American gangs who were influenced by the Black Panther Party and the US organization also proceeded in this progressive political direction by declaring a truce and gang unity. Unfortunately, by the 1980's an avalanche of crack cocaine began to enter Mexican-American and African-American communities and it would prove to be politically and physically deadly. The source of this new lethal drug was documented and exposed in a series of widely-printed articles by journalist Gary Webb of the San Jose Mercury News. His research and facts clearly showed that this heavy flow of crack into these communities was the work of the US-backed Nicaraguan Contras who had been organized by President Reagan and the CIA during the early 1980's and who were using these drug profits from minority communities to buy arms. Webb's detailed reporting which was based upon objective evidence exposed this corrupt alliance and profitable drug operation that would eventually lead to the establishment of large-scale drug gangs and deadly violence which still negatively affect the lives of young minority people. Gary Webb was subsequently targeted by a vicious smear campaign that was organized by right-wing politicians and pro-Reagan newspapers to discredit his reporting and to cover up this Contra drugs-for-arms scandal. This vicious campaign eventually resulted in the loss of Webb's job and subsequently led to his death from two different gunshot wounds to the head which the authorities declared to be a "suicide." This deluge of crack cocaine during the 1980's created an intense competition by young gang members to control and defend this increasingly profitable trade through the acquisition of high-powered weapons and the use of deadly force against one another. The increasing demand for drugs quickly undermined the prevailing gang peace and fueled the formation of new and more violent gang cliques who began to fight for their share of territory, drugs and money. The government policy in reaction to this upsurge in violence and drug consumption was the continuation of [President Richard] Nixon's "War on drugs" which was forcefully implemented by public officials and law enforcement authorities. This policy focused on the effects of the problem by utilizing mass police repression and incarceration rather than gang prevention, intervention and drug rehabilitation. Politically, any previous sense of unity or progressive politics that these gang members were involved in for the betterment of their communities were rapidly submerged by a growing wave of gunfire, violent deaths and widespread drug sales and addiction.

The human potential of these young at-risk persons needs to be salvaged and developed.

A Demand for Drugs Has Transformed Youth Gangs into Thriving Businesses

The increasing demand for drugs within our present society has spawned the growth of thousands of minority youth and adult gangs along with those of white bikers who compete with each other to supply this lucrative market. The profits to be made from this drug trade by young people with a minimal amount of education and few options can be considerable. This whole chain of drug supply and demand has also fueled an arms race to acquire more firepower in order to outgun and overwhelm each gang's competitors and to extend their domination over new drug territory which will further boost their profits. All of this decadent social process has resulted in raising the level of violence and death from gunfire and lethal non-regulated drugs and sharply increasing the number of incarcerated Latinos within the prisons of Texas, New Mexico, Illinois, New York and California. A past era that was somewhat similar to the violent situation that we are experiencing today was Prohibition when liquor was illegal. During this period of history non-Latino ethnic gangs waged vicious battles that killed one another along with innocent bystanders in order to satisfy the public's demand for illegal alcohol and to seize control of its supply and immense profits that it provided. Eventually, the legalization and regulation of alcohol put most of these gangs out of business as the public and government officials finally came to the realization that a sizable number of people in society wanted to drink liquor and that it should be produced safely, legally regulated and taxed. Thus, legalization and regulation finally eliminated the years of violence. Presently, the level of drug consumption and profits, guns and violence and the addiction and imprisonment of Latinos and African-Americans for non-violent drug offenses is spiraling while rehabilitation is lacking. To make matters worse, many of these young people are now beginning to get involved in business alliances with adults from hardcore prison gangs and major drug cartels. This corrosive growth of gangs is causing great harm to the lives of hundreds of thousands of our youth and will eventually impact their children and those around them as well. Gang injunctions and police sweeps along with harsh jail sentences are merely the same failed measures of the past that attempt to put a temporary band-aid on this destructive social activity. Resources are needed to strengthen an intervention strategy of effective drug treatment in conjunction with literacy and job skills training in order to break this growing and corrosive cycle of violence and shattered lives.

Developing the Potential of These Endangered Youths Will Benefit All Latinos

The human potential of these young at-risk persons needs to be salvaged and developed, otherwise their growing presence and unlawful activities will become a social and economic detriment to the well-being of all people within our communities and society as a whole. Many Latinos who have made it to the middle class and feel safe from gang activity in their neighborhoods often tend to dismiss these individuals with sarcastic disdain as simply being cholos or gangbangers. Yet, this sector of troubled youth and the ones now in elementary school who will follow in their footsteps are growing rapidly and will create even more social and educational problems that will affect them directly and the rest of us indirectly. Young people who are members of dysfunctional families, mired in poverty and trapped by inferior educational systems will gravitate toward the allure of gangs and their artificially deceptive and damaging sense of self-esteem, identity, power and money. This cycle of destructive gang activity harms the human potential of young males in addition to a growing number of young girls who are gravitating toward this gang life. Billions are spent on this "war against gangs" which primarily involves the strategy of repression through the use of court ordered gang injunctions, police sweeps and incarceration minus the corrective and necessary alternatives of prevention and rehabilitation. This present policy isn't directed at the cause of the gang problem and is therefore not effective socially nor from a cost standpoint. There are many people who are in denial in regard to this growing gang problem, yet, there is an urgent need to formulate a concrete solution to help resolve this issue. It is our political and ethnic responsibility to support a new approach and policy that clearly focuses on the roots of this social illness that is adversely affecting our youth. Such a policy of early prevention programs should begin in the elementary schools where at-risk children can be identified by trained personnel and steered away from any future involvement with gangs. Such an investment in our youthful human resources will achieve much better results than mere repression and hopefully this will allow all of us to proceed forward in unison and not leave certain unfortunate young people behind.

Heroin Fuels Gang Violence in Chicago

John Lippert, Nacha Cattan, and Mario Parker

John Lippert is a senior writer at Bloomberg Markets. *Nacha Cattan is a reporter for* Bloomberg *based in Mexico. Mario Parker is a reporter for* Bloomberg *based in Chicago.*

The two Mexican couriers were hauling a tractor-trailer full of cash: $3 million collected for drugs sold on the streets of Chicago. Juan Gonzalez and David Zuniga were driving their rig through Indiana in October 2011, transporting the money to Mexico. As they stopped to fix a flat tire, three members of the Gangster Disciples, Chicago's biggest street gang, held them up at gunpoint.

The Mexican Drug Lord of Chicago

The gang had bought the drugs—and now these members wanted the money back. They pistol-whipped and handcuffed Zuniga. As the gangsters were hooking their own purple Kenworth cab to the money-laden trailer, Gonzalez fled through a cornfield and called the police.

After a 15-mile chase north along Interstate 65, lawmen intercepted the rogue truck, arrested the gang members and recovered the loot, *Bloomberg Markets* magazine will report in its October issue.

Gonzalez, who worked for Mexican drug lord Joaquin Guzman, made a surprising request that fall day: He wanted proof for cartel leaders that police had confiscated the $3 million.

"He knew, without a receipt, they'd kill him or his family in Mexico," says Jack Riley, head of the U.S. Drug Enforcement Administration for a five-state region that includes Illinois and Indiana.

Such is the fear that Guzman inspires on both sides of the border. Operating from heavily guarded compounds in the Sierra Madre of northern Mexico, Guzman's Sinaloa cartel supplies 80 percent of the heroin, cocaine, marijuana and methamphetamine—with a street value of $3 billion—that floods the Chicago region each year, the DEA says. Job seekers in Guzman's 150,000-strong enterprise must list where their relatives live.

As far as the authorities can tell, 5-foot 6-inch (1.68-meter) Guzman, a grade school dropout known as El Chapo (or Shorty), has never set foot in Chicago.

Yet during the past seven years, Guzman, who's now in his late 50s, has seized control of the supply and wholesale distribution of drugs in Chicago and much of the Midwest.

This steady flow of dangerous substances is sparking pitched and often deadly turf wars between Chicago's splintered, largely African-American and Latino gangs.

The pipeline of Sinaloa drugs to Chicago runs through the predominantly Mexican neighborhood known as Little Village on the city's southwest side.

"Most of Chicago's violent crime comes from gangs trying to maintain control of drug-selling territories," Riley says. "Guzman supplies a majority of the narcotics that fuel this violence."

Confounding Police

The Department of Justice indicted Guzman in absentia in Chicago in August 2009, charging him with conspiring to transport drugs across international borders. He has so far confounded all efforts by Mexican and U.S. authorities to put him and his cartel out of business. Two years after officers thwarted the Indiana hijacking, police still intercept drugs or cash heading in or out of Chicago every couple of weeks. That pales in comparison to what they miss.

"We're lucky to stop a 10th of what's going through," says Terry Risner, sheriff of Jasper County, Indiana, 80 miles (130 kilometers) southeast of the city.

The pipeline of Sinaloa drugs to Chicago runs through the predominantly Mexican neighborhood known as Little Village on the city's southwest side, authorities say. Yet four years after federal prosecutors indicted twins Margarito and Pedro Flores for being key Guzman distributors in Little Village, police don't know who has succeeded them.

The drugs continue to pour in. In a 2006 conversation monitored by Mexican police, Guzman said he wanted to make America's third-largest city his "home port."

He's done that, says Art Bilek, a retired detective who's executive vice president of the Chicago Crime Commission, a public-safety group that in February named Guzman the city's public enemy No. 1.

"We had freelance distributors in Chicago before," Bilek says. "Guzman has taken them over one by one. He centralized everything—the shipping, warehousing and distribution of drugs, and the collection and transport of money back to Mexico."

Chicago had cartel drugs in the past but not cartel leaders, Bilek says.

"Now, Guzman has top people in here to make sure things run smoothly," he says.

The link between drugs and crime, including violent crime, would be hard to overstate in Chicago. Eighty-six percent of adult males arrested in Chicago last year tested positive for drug use. Chicago, with a population of 2.7 million, had 506 murders in 2012, the highest per capita among the four most populous U.S. cities.

So pervasive is narcotics commerce along the Eisenhower Expressway, the city's main east-west artery, that federal authorities have nicknamed it the Heroin Highway.

The expressway leads to suburban DuPage County, where State's Attorney Robert Berlin recently declared a "heroin epidemic." Since the start of 2012, an average of one heroin user has died every eight-and-a-half days in the county, Berlin says, many of them in their teens and twenties and snorting Sinaloa's product.

As the setting sun casts long shadows on a hot Friday in June, young men in low-riding jeans cluster on porches and around liquor stores near Pulaski Road and Van Buren Street, ready to do business. Keeping an eye out for police, the men lean into car windows, quickly consummating their transactions.

[Chicago] suffers an average of more than five shootings and more than one murder every day.

Gang members pay for their turf with blood. Harold "Noonie" Ward, a leader in the Gangster Disciples before going to jail in 1994 for selling drugs, links the persistence of street violence to Guzman's stranglehold over supply. Ward says Chicago gangs were once able to pick among several Latin American vendors.

Two Chicagos

With Guzman gaining near-monopoly control, they can't negotiate prices: He personally dictates how much distributors pay his operatives, court documents allege. In the past decade, wholesale heroin prices have doubled in Chicago to the current cost of $80,000 a kilogram, says Nick Roti, head of anti-gang enforcement for the city's police. For street sellers to keep profits flowing, they must seize ground in sometimes lethal block-by-block combat.

"The supplier has all the power now; he can set prices," says Ward, 51, who's chief executive officer of Block 8 Productions LLC, a record and film company. "It used to be honor among thieves," he says of gang protocol that punished renegade behavior like the hijacking in Indiana. "Now, it's by any means necessary."

Memorials that have sprung up south and west of downtown reflect a grim statistic: The city suffers an average of more than five shootings and more than one murder every day.

The crimes tell a tale of two Chicagos. The number of murders in the city is half what it was during the crack epidemic of the early 1990s. Yet on portions of the South and West sides, killings are actually more common today, according to research done by Daniel Hertz, a graduate student at the University of Chicago. On the north side, with its parks and high-rise residences abutting Lake Michigan, murders have declined so much that the area now rivals Toronto as an oasis of urban safety, he says.

"Over the last twenty years, at the same time as overall crime has declined, the inequality of violence in Chicago has skyrocketed," Hertz wrote.

The city prepared for another potential bout of bloodshed when schools reopened in late August; After Mayor Rahm Emanuel permanently closed 47 elementary schools in June, mostly in the murder-plagued south and west, the city agreed to hire 600 monitors to escort children through gang boundaries to their new classrooms.

Three days into the academic year, dismissal at one elementary had to be delayed because an 18-year-old woman was shot a few blocks from the school.

Across the street from the community center in Altgeld Gardens, a housing project on the far South Side where President Barack Obama once worked as an organizer, names of gunshot victims line a yellow-brick hallway.

In the South Shore neighborhood, a deflated heart-shaped balloon droops above candles, teddy bears and two white crosses. Police say the victim, 24-year-old Jordan Jefferson, was a Black P. Stone gang member who was on parole for a narcotics violation when he was gunned down on June 30 [2013]. A note written on the wall behind the makeshift shrine reads: "Love you always. RIP. Your Mom."

Eight people were killed during the Labor Day weekend. Four days around the Fourth of July holiday were even bloodier: 47 shootings left 11 people dead, according to the Chicago police. Two boys ran up behind 14-year-old Damani Henard and shot him in the head as he rode the bike he'd received for eighth-grade graduation home from playing video games. Factions of the Four Corner Hustlers are battling over the neighborhood, and Damani was an unintended victim, police say.

"The streets of Chicago belong to gangbangers," says Damani's mother, Yolanda Paige, who, on the day Damani was killed, had made him tacos before leaving for a 16-hour day working two jobs as a nursing assistant.

The biggest driver of violence in Chicago—and where it's becoming difficult to address—is the factionalizing or breaking down of the bigger gangs into . . . smaller cliques.

"We're losing our children," she says.

Guzman grabbed control of Chicago partly by exploiting the disarray among its gangs. From the 1970s into the 2000s, organized mega-gangs divvied up drug-selling territories from public-housing towers, says Jody Weis, a former Federal Bureau of Investigation agent and Chicago Police Department superintendent from 2008 to 2011. The city razed the housing projects just as federal prosecutors were using new racketeering laws to convict and incarcerate gang leaders.

Warring Factions

Rudderless, Chicago's more than 70,000 gang members split into an increasing number of warring factions. When police searched for the reason murders were on a pace to climb past 500 last year, they identified about 625 gang offshoots, including 100 they hadn't previously known about.

"The biggest driver of violence in Chicago—and where it's becoming difficult to address—is the factionalizing or breaking down of the bigger gangs into these smaller cliques," Police Superintendent Garry McCarthy says.

Guzman stepped into the vacuum in Chicago by first winning a key stronghold in Mexico: the transshipment border town of Ciudad Juarez. He was born 300 miles south in the mountain village of La Tuna de Badiraguato, according to Malcolm Beith's "The Last Narco: Inside the Hunt for El Chapo." Relatives sponsored his rise in the drug trade, the book says.

Guzman set his sights on Juarez, a sprawling city of 1.5 million, when cartel leader Amado Carrillo Fuentes died during plastic surgery in 1997.

Incarcerated in a Jalisco, Mexico, prison on murder and drug-trafficking convictions, Guzman escaped in a laundry cart in 2001 and unleashed a spree of assassinations starting seven years later, police say. By 2012, he'd won much of Juarez and the route through El Paso, Texas, and highways north.

A 26-year-old member of the rival Aztec gang recounts those deadly days. Sitting in a sweltering room on a west Juarez street where a table fan strapped to a wooden beam provides no respite from the suffocating heat, the man runs his forefinger under his chin to show how he slit throats.

He recalls how hard it was to sever the arms and legs of one of his victims with a hacksaw because bones are so strong. In all, more than 10,000 people died in the mayhem that cemented Guzman's grip on the Juarez crossing.

Today, Sinaloa hit men and kidnappers called the New People patrol the city, says Alejandro Hope, a former intelligence officer for Mexico's government and now a security analyst at the Mexican Competitiveness Institute. The New People and allied gangs lure recruits—and gain information—with gifts, says the gang member, whose waist swims in his baggy jeans.

Law enforcement officials say Guzman chose Chicago for the same reasons Sears, Roebuck & Co. once centered catalog sales in the city: It's a transportation hub where highways and rail lines converge and then fan across the Midwest.

"They know all of our movements because they're our friends," he says, asking not to be identified because he feared reprisals.

Chicago's connection to Mexican drugs goes back decades. Local Mexican-Americans sold brown heroin called Mexican mud in the 1970s, says Luis Astorga, a sociologist at the National Autonomous University of Mexico. Guzman inherited and improved that network along with channels that Ward, the former Gangster Disciple, says he set up in the early 1990s in Detroit, Minneapolis and elsewhere.

"Logistical Genius"

Law enforcement officials say Guzman chose Chicago for the same reasons Sears, Roebuck & Co. once centered catalog sales in the city: It's a transportation hub where highways and rail lines converge and then fan across the Midwest. The disappearance of factory jobs and the struggle of public schools on the city's South and West sides also give Guzman tens of thousands of willing salesmen who are jobless and poorly educated.

In 2009, a Guzman distributor ran 11 warehouses and stash houses in Chicago and southwestern suburbs. One was in Bedford Park, steps from a facility used by FedEx Corp., operator of the world's largest cargo airline.

"He's a logistical genius and a hands-on guy," Riley says, adding that Guzman is also a billionaire. "If he had turned his talents to legitimate business, he'd probably be in the same situation moneywise."

The Chicago police strategy of saturating high-crime areas with patrols appears to be cutting the homicide rate. Murders through Sept. 8 fell 21 percent—to 297 from 377—from the 2012 period. Yet the authorities have made scant progress in cracking Sinaloa's supply chain.

In January, 70 investigators led by the DEA set up what they call the Chicago Strike Force in a three-story building. One investigation spurred the indictment and arrest of 21 defendants in June for distributing heroin and cocaine in Illinois, Indiana and Wisconsin. Riley expects more arrests, though the narcotics keep flowing.

"The rivers of drugs coming into Chicago are diverse and sufficient to meet demand," says John Hagedorn, a criminologist at the University of Illinois at Chicago. "This is not a war you can win."

Civic leaders and police vowing to reduce the gunfire have homed in on gang-against-gang retribution. On the fifth floor of their South Side headquarters, police use facial-recognition software to scan images from 24,000 city surveillance cameras. Within minutes of a shooting, they send e-mails and texts about gang affiliations—and potential locales for retaliation—so patrols can swarm the trouble spots.

Cure Violence

In the neighborhoods, a Chicago nonprofit called Cure Violence tries to reduce shootings by removing potential attackers and victims from the streets. Frankie Sanchez, a former gang member who works with the group, drove members of the Gangster Two Six Nation, one of Chicago's biggest Latino gangs, to a Wisconsin lake after several shootings in June. After another, he hustled them to the city's Grant Park. The tactic worked: Nobody else got shot, at least not in the critical period immediately following the crimes.

In addition to destroying lives, the violence is bad for business, says Toni Preckwinkle, Cook County Board president.

Skeptics in Mexico say U.S. authorities are defending their own interests by exaggerating Guzman's impact.

"It's terrible for our region because it makes it seem like this is an unsafe place to live and work," she says.

While the city's tourism numbers have held up so far, Moody's Investors Service in July cited crime when it reduced Chicago's general-obligation debt rating by three grades—a magnitude unprecedented for a major U.S. city, according to data since 1990.

"The city's budgetary flexibility is already burdened by high fixed costs, including unrelenting public safety demands," analysts wrote.

Skeptics in Mexico say U.S. authorities are defending their own interests by exaggerating Guzman's impact.

"It's easier to sell the need for a bump in your budget if you speak about evil Mexicans than if you present a complex web of gangs," says Hope, the Mexican Competitiveness Institute analyst.

In Chicago, the DEA-led strike force concentrates its anti-Guzman efforts in Little Village, where immigrants have congregated for a century.

On a sunny June afternoon, traffic snarls on 26th Street as diners enjoy tortillas and roast pork at $25 for four people. The Two-Six gang takes its name from this thoroughfare, which is lined with currency exchanges for buying identification cards and wiring cash back to Mexico.

Guzman keeps the price of cocaine artificially high to push a more profitable and easily transportable product his chemists refined—a snortable heroin that lures suburbanites wary of needles.

The DEA is zeroing in on so-called choke points in Little Village where drugs change hands between distributors and street gangs.

"The middlemen tend to be Mexican gang members from the Latin Kings, Two-Six and Maniac Latin Disciples," says Roti of the Chicago police. "From there, it flows to African-American gangs, who control the street."

Luis Lopez says he's proud to be a Two-Six member. Since grade school, he says, he never wanted to do anything but join members of his extended family in the gang. From the sidelines of a softball game in July, Lopez, 18, describes the links between Little Village and Mexican smuggling.

"Since we're Latino, we know more people who are tied to the cartel," he says. "The black guys, they need us for drugs and guns because we have the right connection."

The top-ranked Sinaloa operatives in Little Village are obsessed with secrecy, criminologist Hagedorn says. They deal whenever possible with family members and have no interest in leading a Chicago gang.

"Why would you want that hassle when you're busy making money?" he asks.

Little Village police commander Maria Pena understands how gangs operate after growing up in nearby Logan Square.

"In my district, Latinos are more territorial than gangs in other parts of the city," says Pena, a 25-year veteran who once walked a beat. "They won't allow opposition gangs to come through. They only sell drugs to known individuals."

A few blocks north of Little Village, black gangs peddle Sinaloa drugs near the Eisenhower Expressway, the Heroin Highway. Riley says Guzman keeps the price of cocaine artificially high to push a more profitable and easily transportable product his chemists refined—a snortable heroin that lures suburbanites wary of needles.

"They think if they snort or smoke it, they won't end up injecting," says R. Gil Kerlikowske, director of the Office of National Drug Control Policy. "Very quickly, they do."

Flores Twins

The Flores twins in Little Village were the cornerstones of Guzman's U.S. business from 2005 to 2008, federal court documents allege. They took delivery of 2,000 kilograms (4,400 pounds) of cocaine a month from Sinaloa and associated cartels, plus heroin, the documents say. Their trafficking approached $700 million in 2008.

The twins used local warehouses to break down loads from Mexico for retail distribution around Chicago and shipment as far away as Vancouver. They encoded ledgers to track cash sent to Mexico for drugs purchased on credit and to note which couriers handled each step of the process.

The system ran smoothly until early 2008. Guzman began a war with boyhood friend Arturo Beltran Leyva over, among other things, the loyalty of the Flores brothers, according to federal court documents. As the Guzman-Beltran Leyva battle claimed hundreds of lives in Mexico, the twins offered during the summer of 2008 to help the DEA investigate Guzman,

Patrick Fitzgerald, then-U.S. attorney for the Northern District of Illinois, said in court documents.

The twins recorded their phone calls with Guzman and their visits to his mountain stronghold. In an October 2008 meeting that included Margarito Flores, Guzman and subordinates complained that Mexican authorities had ceded power to the U.S. in the war on drugs.

"They are f—ing us everywhere," he said. In a taped phone call in November 2008, he approved Pedro Flores's request for a 9 percent drop in the charge for Chicago heroin—to $50,000 a kilogram—citing poor quality.

"That price is fine," Guzman said.

The Flores twins also taped Jesus Vicente Zambada Niebla, son of Ismael Zambada, who court documents identify as a principal Sinaloa leader along with Guzman. Mexican soldiers arrested the younger Zambada in March 2009. He was extradited to Chicago, where he's awaiting trial on drug-trafficking-conspiracy charges. He pleaded not guilty on all counts. Charges against the Flores twins are still pending.

Police deconstructed a further piece of Guzman's Chicago network with the August 2010 arrest of Erik Guevara, whom they say has family ties to Sinaloa in Mexico.

Sinaloa leaders orchestrate punishments from afar. In 2011, they sent a list of targets to a clan of Chicago roofers who served as cartel enforcers by night.

They charged Guevara, 31, with conspiracy to supply heroin after discovering a secret compartment under the floor of a house in suburban Forest Park, Illinois, court records allege.

The building had been owned by an 86-year-old woman who died five years earlier. Guevara, who lived nearby, appropriated the vacant home to stash money and drugs. He was arrested in 2010 with 7.7 kilograms of heroin stuffed in a drive shaft he was transporting in his Jeep, the Justice Department says. He pleaded guilty and began a 30-year jail sentence in January.

Sinaloa leaders orchestrate punishments from afar. In 2011, they sent a list of targets to a clan of Chicago roofers who served as cartel enforcers by night, says John Blair, intelligence director for the Cook County Sheriff's Office. The dossier contained names of people Guzman's cartel believed had robbed it in Mexico.

Blair suspects roofer Arturo Ibarra was among Guzman's U.S. hit men. Police shot and killed Ibarra as he fled from a north side neighborhood just as two men named in the dossier lay bleeding to death from stab wounds.

The Gangster Disciples who tried to hijack Guzman's cash in 2011 have avoided Sinaloa reprisals so far, says Jasper County prosecutor Kathryn O'Neall. An Indiana judge sentenced the trio on May 28 to three years in prison for money laundering. Gonzalez and Zuniga, who cooperated with authorities, weren't charged.

Guzman's grip on the U.S. Midwest may actually be strengthened by a move Mexican authorities hailed as a victory in their war on trafficking. In July, they arrested Miguel Angel Trevino Morales, head of the Zetas cartel, which Sinaloa has been battling over a route through Nuevo Laredo on the U.S. border.

"Trevino's arrest makes it easier for Sinaloa to conquer territory," says Jorge Chabat, a security analyst at the Mexico City-based Center for Economic Research and Teaching.

The reach of Sinaloa and its elusive leader extends from the rugged Sierra Madre to the dusty streets of Juarez to Chicago and beyond.

"They're the pre-eminent organized crime group in the world today," the Chicago Police Department's Roti says. "They have almost unlimited resources."

Drug Warriors and Gun Violence

James Peron

James Peron is the president of the Moorfield Storey Institute, an independent think tank dedicated to equality of rights before the law, social tolerance, and civil liberties. He has written for numerous publications, including the Wall Street Journal *(Europe),* Reason, *and* The Johannesburg Star. *He is the author of* Zimbabwe: Death of a Dream.

D rugs can kill users. Drug warriors can kill anybody.

Violence Leads to Violence

A CBS report on street violence in Chicago makes clear that a major cause—if not *the* major cause—of these deaths is because drug gangs are fighting over turf. Jack Riley, the DEA [Drug Enforcement Agency] chief for Chicago, says that he is absolutely sure that most of the gun deaths are part of the fight for drug turf.

This is absolutely true and drug warriors like Jack Riley are responsible for the fight.

Consider what Riley considers a success for drug warriors: the arrest of drug dealers and the confiscation of their product.

What exactly does this success do? If they are successful enough to reduce the street supply of drugs they increase the price of drugs. The first thing that happens is that they give windfall profits to all the dealers who they didn't arrest. They didn't hurt those dealers, they rewarded them.

Second, the increased profits make drug dealing more attractive.

Riley and his crew strap on their SWAT outfits, prepared for battle. They're armed, dangerous and prepared to kill. The DEA is willing to use war-like violence.

This will drive out peaceful dealers and the more placid distributors. But with massive profits created by the DEA all they do is attract more and more violent dealers to the market.

The more violent the DEA is willing to be, the more violent the dealers will be. We don't see beer distributors killing for "turf," at least not anymore. But, when we allowed the Jack Rileys of the country to set liquor laws from 1920 to 1933 we had violence, gang warfare and murder. When Prohibition was repealed and liquor legalized the violence stopped.

We still have alcoholics, but their addiction isn't a crime. They aren't forced to deal with criminal gangs to get what they want.

Drug users risk their lives, but even a good deal of that is due to impure drugs with varying qualities—directly attributable to the illegality of the drugs themselves. If you take heroin, however, that in itself does not risk the lives of others.

The DEA is acting like just another rival drug gang. They propel their competitors, the other drug gangs, to match them in violence.

Drug warriors regularly raid the wrong homes and sometimes shoot innocent people. At least the drug dealers don't pretend they are a force for good. You can't say that for drug warriors.

They are sanctimonious and self-righteous. They are convinced that their tanks, SWAT raids, concussion grenades and assault rifles, which they regularly point at their fellow citizens, are signs of their righteousness. They are really signs of everything that is wrong with the war on drugs.

Another Gang

The DEA is acting like just another rival drug gang. They propel their competitors, the other drug gangs, to match them in violence. They raise the stakes—and the dealers see them and raise them again.

The way to destroy the drug gang violence is to take the profit out of it. The Drug Warriors know that, they just don't understand the most basic principles of economics. They think that they take the profit out by reducing the supply. That is entirely foolish. Reducing the supply, without touching the demand, only raises the profits.

End the war on drugs and legalize the product and profits plummet, the cost of drugs decline. Users would no longer have to deal with street gangs. Of course, the DEA thugs will be out of a job. The war on drugs also profits the DEA and the local drug warriors. They get billions in funding, decent salaries, and the adrenaline rushes they are addicted to. They, and the bureaucrats who profit from the war on drugs, will fight attempts to treat drug use as a medical problem, instead of a criminal one.

Portugal decriminalized drugs and treats users as individuals who need help, not as criminals. Drug related deaths dropped as a result.

As bad as drugs can be, Drug Warriors are worse. They raise the stakes of the drug fight, incentivize the drug gangs and push them to greater heights of violence. Then these pious frauds storm in, guns blazing, Constitutional rights being shredded, and high on the rush they get from their violence. They pat themselves on the backs and pretend they are making America a better place.

When a solution becomes worse than the problem it is time to abolish the solution. The gun violence in Chicago is directly linked to the incentives created by the war on drugs. Ending the war on drugs will do more to end gun violence in America than any other policy change we can implement. But it is the only solution that the Drug Warriors, on both sides of the aisle, won't contemplate.

CHAPTER 2

Are Gangs and Gang Violence Increasing in the United States?

Chapter Preface

Discussions of violence in the United States often focus on issues such as guns and drugs, both of which are linked to gang activity. However, some researchers have argued that the main reason for changes in violence in America is due to an entirely different factor—lead exposure.

The theory that lead is responsible for changes in violent crime has been around for some time. One of its chief proponents is economist Rick Nevin, whose work is profiled in a July 8, 2007, article by Shankar Vedantam. Nevin argued that the 67 percent reduction in homicides and 57 percent reduction in crime in New York City from 1994 to 2001 was not the result of mayor Rudy Giuliani's policing strategies; rather, Nevin said, violence decreased because of long-term city, state, and federal efforts to reduce lead in paint and gasoline. When infants exposed to lead grow up to be adolescents, they are more likely to be impulsive and aggressive. Cleaning up lead in the 1970s and 1980s has resulted in a steady drop in crime in the United States (including New York City) from the 1990s to the present.

Kevin Drum, in a 2013 article in *Mother Jones*, expanded on the argument for the importance of lead. Drum pointed out that the broad pattern of violent crime seems to follow the rise and fall of the use of leaded gasoline in America. Lead was added to gasoline in the early 1940s and increased through the early 1970s, before being phased out in subsequent decades. Crime rates, for their part, rose from the 1960s through the 1990s, before starting to fall—a pattern consistent with Nevin's theory that infant exposure to lead would lead to increased crime in adolescence, fifteen or twenty years after exposure. Drum thus concluded that the best crime prevention program would be a systematic investment in lead abatement, which could reduce crime as much as 10 percent, producing savings of as much as $150 billion a year. Drum argued that violence is dropping, and that the way to make it drop even more is to focus, not on gangs, but on lead.

The following chapter looks at arguments about the prevalence of gang violence in America, focusing on such issues as the benefits of policing, the effects of social media, and some cities where gang violence has increased or decreased.

Social Media Has Led to an Increase in Gang Violence

Ben Austen

Ben Austen is a reporter and writer for Wired *and other magazines.*

Last year more than 500 people were murdered in Chicago, a greater number than in far more populous cities such as New York and Los Angeles. The prevalence of gun crimes in Chicago is due in large part to a fragmentation of the gangs on its streets: There are now an estimated 70,000 members in the city, spread out among a mind-boggling 850 cliques, with many of these groupings formed around a couple of street corners or a specific school or park. Young people in these areas are like young people everywhere, using technology to coordinate with their friends and chronicle their every move. But in neighborhoods where shootings are common, the use of online tools has turned hazardous, as gang violence is now openly advertised and instigated online.

Facebook Drillers

We naturally associate criminal activity with secrecy, with conspiracies hatched in alleyways or back rooms. Today, though, foolish as it may be in practice, street gangs have adopted a level of transparency that might impress even the most fervent Silicon Valley futurist. Every day on Facebook and Twitter, on Instagram and YouTube, you can find unabashed teens flashing hand signs, brandishing guns, splaying out drugs and wads of cash. If we live in an era of openness, no segment of the population is more surprisingly open than 21st-century gang members, as they simultaneously document and roil the streets of America's toughest neighborhoods.

There's a term sometimes used for a gangbanger who stirs up trouble online: Facebook driller. He rolls out of bed in the morning, rubs his eyes, picks up his phone. Then he gets on Facebook and starts insulting some person he barely knows, someone in a rival crew. It's so much easier to do online than face-to-face. Soon someone else takes a screenshot of the post and starts passing it around. It's one thing to get cursed out in front of four or five guys, but online the whole neighborhood can see it—the whole city, even. So the target has to retaliate just to save face. And at that point, the quarrel might be with not just the Facebook driller a few blocks away but also haters 10 miles north or west who responded to the post. What started as a provocation online winds up with someone getting drilled in real life. . . .

Not *The Wire*

[There is a] fundamental shift in how gangs operate, both here in Chicago and around the country. Harold Pollack, codirector of the University of Chicago Crime Lab, says that in every talk he gives about gangs, someone inevitably asks him about [television drama] *The Wire*—wanting to know who is, say, the Stringer Bell of Chicago.

> *Increasingly, disagreements that end in bloodshed have their origins online.*

But *The Wire*, based in part on David Simon's Baltimore crime reporting in the 1980s and '90s, is now very dated in its depiction of gangs as organized crime syndicates. For one thing, Stringer Bell would never let his underlings advertise their criminal activities, as a Central Florida crew did this spring when it posted on its public Facebook page that two of its members had violated their parole and been arrested for posing with guns on their personal Facebook pages. Even a few years ago, a member of, say, the Disciples would have been "violated"—physically punished—for talking about killings or publicly outing a fellow member. But today most "gangs" are without much hierarchical structure, and many of the cliques are only nominally tied to larger organizations.

Similarly, the majority of the violence isn't strategic but results instead from petty personal exchanges. Young people in embattled Chicago neighborhoods are scared and heavily armed—police seize more guns than the NYPD and LAPD combined, an average of 130 illegal firearms each week. "A couple of young guys, plus a disagreement, plus guns equals dead body," Pollack says bluntly. "These are stupid 17-year-old homicides. That's the extent of it today."

Increasingly, disagreements that end in bloodshed have their origins online. The Chicago police department, which now patrols social media along with the streets, estimates that an astonishing 80 percent of all school disturbances result from online exchanges. . . .

The Online Gangosphere

Even for an outsider, the online gangosphere isn't difficult to enter. Sites like TheHoodUp.com and StreetGangs.com host message boards where gangsters openly swap tips and tricks: how much an ounce of weed is worth, how to bribe a cop or judge. Videos from ChiTownBangn and Gang Bang City Ent. look like the thug-life version of *Girls Gone Wild* [adult entertainment company that creates DVDs], the cameras inspiring kids to act out vicious caricatures of themselves. WorldStarHipHop.com has become a clearinghouse for amateur fight videos, with guys often shouting "WorldStar!" as they record themselves administering beatings or film someone else being pummeled; the site even puts together best-of-the-week fight compilations.

On YouTube, search for the name of any gang or clique, or better yet the name plus "killa" ("Vice Lord Killa," "Latin Kings Killa"), and you can quickly find yourself on just about any block in gangland America. In these videos, guys proudly proclaim their allegiance into the camera, shouting out tributes to their gang and even announcing their own names and aliases. People in the videos often light up a joint or flash a gun tucked in their waistband while bragging to the camera that they know the police are watching.

As with the gangs themselves, though, the gangland videos often sit on a blurry line between criminality and sociality. The goal is really to display a strength in numbers and firepower—an image seen by foes a few streets away as well as by the next generation of kids on the block. On YouTube, you'll find thousands of amateur rap videos that seem to double as gang videos, with rappers giving shout-outs to the various cliques in their neighborhood, their friends stepping into the background—or the foreground—to show off a gun and act crazy. The YouTube video for "WildEnd We Out Here," a hip hop track by an 18-year-old named Yung Killa, or YK, opens with an anarchic late-night party scene in the city's legendary Cabrini-Green housing project. As YK name-checks each gang, we see its members joyously throwing up their crooked finger signs.

Gang enforcement officers in Chicago started looking closely at social media sites about three years ago, after learning that high school students were filming fights in the hallways and alcoves of their schools and posting the videos online.

Not long ago I met up with Yung Killa, whose real name is Devonta Hodge, and Deandra Howell, a 20-year-old who goes by Lil Dre Day. WildEnd refers to both the section of Cabrini-Green where they're from and their rap collective, WildEnd

Entertainment. We speak in my car, parked in the lot of a Pizza Hut along the Dan Ryan Expressway on Chicago's far South Side. "Social media is going to put you out there, but it's not all going to be pretty," Howell says from the passenger seat. And while they self-identify as onetime gangbangers, the two young men insist that their YouTube videos are like crafted "movie skits" and aren't intended to glorify (let alone provoke) acts of violence. Their current goal is to make it onto MTV or BET's *106th&Park*. But the songs do draw inspiration from their lives in the projects, where gangs and guns and extreme poverty are the everyday reality; just a few months prior, their manager was shot to death as he sat right beside them. . . .

Peering over my shoulder from the backseat, Hodge asks why the name Ryda Gang is written in my notebook. I tell him that I watched a couple of Ryda Gang videos on YouTube. In one of them, a group of young men are parked outside the Cabrini row houses as they film themselves in a black minivan at night. "Curfew time!" someone yells out, as others appear along the narrow strip, Hodge among them. A person from the van announces into the camera that he's affiliated with the Black Disciples. Another one, describing himself as a gang veteran, zeroes in on the five blue-light surveillance cameras that surround the block, detailing for anyone with an Internet connection his plans to cut the wires on one of them. Apparently he doesn't like to be watched.

"Ryda Gang is a *gang* gang," Hodge says, stressing each word as if willing me to comprehend. "WildEnd is a music group." But . . . on the Internet especially it's hard to differentiate between the two. . . .

Policing Social Media

The headquarters of the Chicago police department is on the South Side, a couple of blocks from where the White Sox play and not far from where the Robert Taylor Homes, once the country's largest housing project, stood until they were torn down nearly a decade ago. On the day I visit the station, 20 recruits who have just completed their training line up in front of a mural of the neighborhood, preparing to be sworn in for duty. I sit down in a folding chair near Kevin Ryan, commander of the gang enforcement unit, and Ken Boudreau, a 27-year department veteran who runs the gang unit's school-safety team. Over his protruding belly, Boudreau wears a worn bulletproof vest, its Velcro straps frayed and discolored. On the seat beside him, he places a BlackBerry and a second phone, each emitting constant chirps. Ryan, in a brown pin-striped suit and trim mustache, takes an iPad from his brief-case. He's reluctant to talk too specifically about the methods they use to monitor the online activity of gangbangers, for fear of limiting his capabilities. But he assures me that I could figure out most of it just by tooling around with a few search terms. On his iPad, he types "CPDK," for Chicago Police Department Killers, and shows me the string of results on You-Tube, guys crowing in each video about their desire to kill cops. Gang enforcement officers in Chicago started looking closely at social media sites about three years ago, after learning that high school students were filming fights in the hall-ways and alcoves of their schools and posting the videos on-line. Boudreau tells me that they began to hear about fight videos going on YouTube during the day, and then they would often see a related shooting later in the afternoon. In the department's deployment operations center, the other unit in the force that regularly monitors social media activity, officers first took notice when they read in the newspaper about a West Side gang member who was using the Internet to find out about enemies being released from prison. But "virtual policing" became a priority only after kids aligned with local cliques started calling each other out in rap videos.

Much of this police work is reactive. In the same way that flyers taped to light poles used to announce parties, news of a big gathering is now posted online, and officers move into position based on that intel. Other times guys will say point-blank that they're going to kill someone. "We're like, oh shit, we better put some police there because this is about to set off," an officer in deployment operations says. When people brag about a crime they've already committed, detectives use that as yet another investigative tool, assuming that online admissions alone won't hold up in court. (Though in one successful case, a Cincinnati district attorney was able to introduce thousands of pieces of online evidence of suspects appearing beside guns, drugs, and one another to establish a criminal conspiracy.)

The public nature of social media gives police and advocacy groups some warning about trouble before it starts.

But over time, the cops' approach to social media has become more entrepreneurial. The police in Chicago now actively look for inflammatory comments around specific dates: the anniversary of a homicide, say, or the birthday of a slain gang member, the sorts of events that have often incited renewed rounds of violence. They also use information collected from public sites to add to their knowledge about the hundreds of cliques and sets operating in the city, cataloging the members, affiliations, beefs, and geographic boundaries.

"We saved a life this week," Boudreau says. A middle-school student from Englewood had denigrated Chief Keef [a locally known rapper and gangster] and the Black Disciples in a rap video. Looking at the comments, Boudreau's team could see that Keef partisans were mobilizing; the online taunts were close to spilling over into real-world violence. The police notified the 12-year-old's family, and he and a classmate were relocated from the neighborhood. The next day the police spotted the rivals prowling near the boy's home. It was the same story as JoJo's [a rapper who was killed after an altercation with Keef], Boudreau says, except with a different ending.

Anticipating Crimes

Police and other experts say the ad hoc, emotional nature of street violence today might actually present an opportunity. Repairing big rifts between warring criminal enterprises is really hard; defusing minor beefs and giving kids skills to regulate their socio-emotional behavior is highly labor-intensive but effective. And the public nature of social media gives police and advocacy groups some warning about trouble before it starts. For a long time, criminal-justice experts have talked about predictive policing—the idea that you can use big data to sniff out crimes before they happen, conjuring up an ethically troublesome future like the one depicted in Steven Spielberg's [2002 film] *Minority Report*. But in Chicago and other big cities, police are finding it's much easier than that. Give people social media and they'll tell you what they're about to do.

Just as Chicago cops helped save that 12-year-old in Englewood, police departments around the country are trying to use information gleaned from online posts to anticipate crimes and prevent them from ever taking place. In Cincinnati, officers at the police department's real-time crime center track dozens of sites daily in a room filled with video monitors. Captain Dan Gerard, who runs the unit, says they want gangbangers to know that the police are watching. A beat cop can bait a suspect who passes on the street: *I know you were out celebrating last night; I know who you were with.* "It's designed to get in their heads, to rattle them, so they put the guns down," Gerard says.

In New York City, where the number of homicides is now the lowest since it started keeping crime statistics 50 years ago, the NYPD credits much of its recent success to monitoring online gang activity. The department determined that street-crew members, by and large teenagers, were responsible for a vastly disproportionate share of the violent crimes in the city. And so last year it launched Operation Crew Cut, which is doubling the number of detectives in its gang division to 300, with many of the additional officers focusing specifically on social media sites. The result, authorities say, has been a steep drop in retaliatory violence, as the police have been able to identify clashes and step in before they escalate. "Any tweet might hold the identities of the next potential victim and per-petrator," NYPD deputy commissioner Paul Browne says.

There are some signs in Chicago too that police and com-munity efforts might be working. Compared with its pace in 2012, the homicide rate this year has decreased. But as of mid-August [2013], there were still more than 220 people murdered and 1,000 shot; 47 shootings occurred over the July 4 holiday weekend alone. The daily scorekeeping itself has turned into a grim yardstick, a gauge of the quality of life in a place where life is valued far too cheaply.

Detroit Is Experiencing an Epidemic of Gang Violence

James A. Buccellato

James A. Buccellato is a professor of history at Wayne State University in Detroit, Michigan.

As anyone who's tuned in the news lately [2013] knows, crime reduction is a primary goal of Detroit mayoral candidates Mike Duggan and Benny Napoleon. Both have crime fighting credentials: Duggan was a Wayne County Prosecutor while Benny Napoleon served as Wayne County Sheriff.

Gangs and Detroit

Each candidate recognizes the epidemic of violent crime in the Motor City. Registering almost 400 homicides in 2012, Detroit ranks as one of America's most violent cities. These statistics are particularly alarming considering that national crime rates are on the decline. According to FBI measurements, 2012 violent crime rates were 12.9 percent lower than 2008 and 12.2 percent lower than 2003 levels. Yet as national crime rates trend down, Detroit's violent crime levels are on the rise.

Tragically, Detroit's youth often find themselves at the center of street violence. In 2010, for example, the city registered 106 youth homicides while apprehending 12,000 young people for criminal activities.

When law enforcement examines this problem they often find gangs at the nexus of youth violence. The National Gang Threat Assessment (NGTA) report, for example, indicates that almost 50 percent of violent crimes are gang related. The report also notes there are 1.4 million active "street, outlaw motorcycle gang, and prison gang members" in the United States. Overall, there are 33,000 gangs within the United States, a 40% increase from 2009.

But what is the situation in Detroit? Is there a strong correlation between street gangs and youth violence in the Motor City?

Providing an answer is difficult, as experts rarely agree on what we mean by the term "gang." Researching Chicago gangs in the 1920s, sociologist Frederic Thrasher observed that "no two gangs are alike." Today, most social scientists agree with Thrasher and categorize gangs into different typologies, assigning gangs varying degrees of criminality.

From law enforcement's perspective, however, the gang is primarily an organized criminal entity. The NGTA report breaks the gang into four categories: street, prison, outlaw motorcycle, and neighborhood. Researchers refer to the top layer of criminal gangs as "corporate gangs." Such gangs maintain vertical structures and operationally resemble ethnic criminal organizations like the Italian mafia.

Over the years, Detroit produced a number of infamous corporate gangs with colorful names like the Purple Gang and YBI (Young Boys Incorporated). While the Purples dominated the bootleg trade during Prohibition, YBI sold copious amounts of cocaine during the 1980s.

Experts agree that Detroit's gangs are primarily neighborhood based, rather than franchises in some national crime network.

In recent years a handful of Detroit based corporate gangs emerged as major players in the narcotics trade and federal law enforcement acted accordingly. In 2003, the Drug Enforcement Administration busted up the Puritan Avenue drug ring for running multistate cocaine operations. Two years later, federal agents took down the Black Mafia Family (BMF) for running a multimillion dollar cocaine empire.

And in June, 2013 the U.S. Attorney's Office sentenced the leader of the Hustle Boys to thirty years in prison for witness tampering and trafficking prescription pain pills in multiple states.

Neighborhood Cliques

Though corporate gangs grab newspaper headlines, researchers find that such gangs are uncommon in the Motor City. Experts agree that Detroit's gangs are primarily neighborhood based, rather than franchises in some national crime network.

Unlike the hierarchical gangs of Chicago, or the institutionalized gangs of Los Angeles, Detroit gangs form around smaller neighborhood cliques. And unlike Chicago and Los Angeles, the gang situation is fluid in the Motor City.

"A new gang starts every week, while another dissolves" comments Lyle Dungy of the Detroit Crime Commission. Dungy is a Marine and retired Detroit Police officer and served on the Department's Organized Crime Task Force. He adds that while there are a few national brand name gangs like the Latin Counts in Southwest Detroit, most local gangs revolve around a school district or some other neighborhood affiliation. That doesn't mean they are any less violent, but are organic formations rather than the product of some centralized national conspiracy.

In terms of involvement in the drug trade, Dungy notes that "Dirty Sprite" is the chic drug with today's neighborhood gangs. The drink is prescription codeine syrup that party goers mix with soft drinks like Sprite. "On the streets, the syrup can go for $800 a bottle or $40 a line" comments Dungy.

While a local gang member may find the prescription drug business lucrative, it is very different from the vertically integrated distribution systems run by nationally syndicated gangs. According to local film-maker Al Profit, the notion of the corporate gang is obsolete in the Motor City. Profit has documented the issue of crime in Detroit through such films as Rollin and Motown Mafia. He maintains that today, the combination of RICO (Racketeer Influenced and Corrupt Organizations) laws and "draconian mandatory sentencing makes it impossible to build an organization of the same magnitude as YBI." Ironically, neighborhoods are in some ways more dangerous when the gang situation is fluid and decentralized. According to Profit, during the 1980s and 1990s "working people were involved in these larger gang operations and as result there was a code on the streets." For example, organizations like YBI would "keep stick-up guys out of the neighborhood, keep breaking and entering to a minimum, and make sure the grass was cut." Researchers still see some of this code in Southwest Detroit with brand name gangs like the Latin Counts. "These gangs are smarter, they keep violence to a minimum so as to avoid police surveillance," adds Dungy.

Today with cell phones and laptops drug gangs can arrange dope drops and buys anywhere anytime.

Spatially the game has changed for Detroit gangs as well. While the neighborhood is the nexus of gang activity, cyberspace is increasingly important terrain for violent youth. "They tweet, update Facebook, and circulate videos on Youtube," comments Dungy. In many cases, gang members use social media to discuss past crimes and openly display contraband.

Although Detroit gangs tend to form organically, researchers note that because of the internet, a few local gangs are adopting national brand names. Such gangs are not franchises though. Instead, young individuals see the ubiquity of gang visuals streaming across social media and adopt national brands accordingly. "We see local gangs affiliated with Money Over Everything," a gang traditionally found in the American South comments Dungy.

Also, some neighborhood gangs on Detroit's East side, a hot zone for youth violence, claim affiliation with the Bloods.

In terms of territory, multimedia technology is also changing the drug game. Profit explains that "back in the day a street corner may generate $10,000 a day in drug sales. But today with cell phones and laptops drug gangs can arrange dope drops and buys anywhere anytime."

Joining Gangs to Survive

For community activist Yusef Shakur, however, the socioeconomic environment in Detroit is the key to understanding today's youth violence. Shakur is a former member of the Zone 8 gang. Today he is a political writer and is involved in community empowerment projects like the Urban Network. In terms of gang activity, "there is a direct relationship to lack of opportunities" explains Shakur. He adds that young people join gangs "out of survival."

According to the Social Science Research Council, Detroit "has the highest youth unemployment rate (30 percent) and adult unemployment rate (17 percent) of any of the twenty-five largest metro areas." Furthermore, "The data show that education is far less an obstacle in Detroit than diminished opportunities to enter the workforce."

Significantly, the Council finds that the "disconnection" between youth and employment is concentrated in the African American community. The report notes that "Detroit's African American youth have disconnection rates of 25.3 percent, as compared with 13.5 percent of whites and 19.2 percent of Latinos."

According to Shakur, the problem of youth violence is not just an economic issue. "We shouldn't talk about at-risk youth, we should talk about at-risk communities." He argues there is a correlation between underdeveloped economic conditions and declining social capital. Today's youth (inner-city and otherwise) no longer find traditional forms of community authority, such as the church, labor union, and local school efficacious. As a result, they seek meaning and self-identity in the gang. "T-Stones, Boys' Town, 12th Street . . . these are today's agents of socialization" laments Shakur.

This search for identity explains the fetishization of cyberspace by today's youth. There is real social currency to "being seen and heard" through social media. Ultimately there is no point being in a neighborhood gang if no one knows.

The forecast for youth violence is bleak according to Shakur. With failing social institutions and few economic opportunities, some Detroit neighborhoods resemble "Third World conditions." Shakur refers to such neighborhoods as "Zombieland." And politically there is no urban agenda at the national level.

Locally, however, the City of Detroit has a "Youth Violence Prevention Strategy." Although the policy does not address poverty, it does include a "comprehensive anti-gang initiative." Part of the City's larger initiative includes a $100 million Skillman Good Neighborhoods grant. The grant emphasizes education and community betterment programs.

Meanwhile, in August, 2013 the Detroit Crime Commission persuaded Detroit PD to reinstitute "the gang squad." In terms of joint federal and local policy, the Eastern District Court recently unveiled "Operation Cease Fire." The initiative is a $1.5 million grant that includes a combination of law enforcement and social assistance.

As for the mayoral candidates, each highlights his crime fighting qualifications. Napoleon reminds voters that he led the Detroit PD Gang Unit that battled notorious drug organizations like the Chambers Brothers. Duggan, meanwhile, reminds voters that as Wayne County Prosecutor he shut down "over 900 drug houses" in Detroit.

Overall, Shakur argues that going after gangs is "too easy." Until policy makers and community leaders address economic development and declining social capital, the gangs of Detroit will persevere.

Gang Violence Is Increasing in Denver

Sadie Gurman

Sadie Gurman is a reporter at The Denver Post *covering several Colorado police departments, public safety, and other aspects of the criminal justice system. She has also worked at the* Pittsburgh Post-Gazette *and the* Rockford Register Star.

The number of gang-related violent crimes in Denver has nearly doubled in the first four months of this year, despite a police program aimed at encouraging gangsters to lead more peaceful lives.

Ceasefire Program

The overall number of gang-related or gang-motivated offenses has remained nearly steady in the first four months of this year [2013] compared with 2012, but police department figures show an increased percentage of violent gang-related crimes. Aggravated assaults, for example, have more than doubled, from 47 between Jan. 1 and April 22, 2012, to 107 during the same period this year. In the first four months of 2012, there were 72 gang-related crimes against people; in that same period this year there have been 132.

Police officials say it is too soon to gauge the success of the far-reaching Ceasefire program and that the numbers don't tell the entire story.

But Dianne Cooks, whose son was paralyzed in a gang-related shooting in 2005, said the program has not gone far enough to curb gang violence.

"It's not working yet," said Cooks, director of Families Against Violent Acts. "It ain't going down. And it's getting warmer, so we don't know what's going to happen now. I think it's going to get worse."

Ceasefire, unrolled in October, enlists law enforcement, community leaders and clergy to gather gang members in closed-door meetings, where they demand the violence end and promise steep punishment if it doesn't. Social services then offer a path toward reform through job-placement programs, rehab and counseling.

The approach has been tried in other cities with varying results, but it has also proved difficult to sustain. It is based on an effort credited for slashing Boston's homicide rate by nearly 70 percent in the mid-1990s. But about six years after the program launched in that city, gang slayings reached a 10-year high.

Denver police Chief Robert White has said Ceasefire resembles a plan he implemented as police chief in Greensboro. N.C., where officials say it led to a 51 percent drop in violent crime since 2000.

[Denver police] have classified at least five of this year's 19 homicides as gang-related or -motivated.

"The first six months are important, but it takes longer than that," said Dwight Crotts, deputy police chief in Greensboro, where the program got off to a similarly slow start. "The long-term impact of that won't be felt before a year or so."

Cooks said she was hopeful about the initiative when, as part of it, she stood in front of a room full of gang members and shared with them a mother's perspective on the effects of their violence. But she said she has not been satisfied with the results.

Police have classified at least five of this year's 19 homicides as gang-related or -motivated. There had been three such killings at this time last year.

Gangs have been behind some of this year's most troubling cases, including the Jan. 16 shooting of District 1 Sgt. Robert Motyka during a police chase and gunbattle on the northwest side. An argument between rival gang members touched off a shooting that wounded three during last month's 4/20 marijuana smokeout [a pro-pot rally] in a packed Civic Center.

And an 8-year-old boy remains hospitalized after someone fired shots into the Jeep he was riding in on April 29 in southwest Denver, hitting him in the back. The city's gang unit is investigating that case.

Too Early for Results

"I'm troubled by the shootings," White said. "But I'm confident about the program. It's just too early right now. It's hard to make an assessment of the effectiveness of how the program has been."

The success of the program should be measured in ways other than hard data, White said. And Cmdr. Marc Fleecs, who oversees the program for the department, said the effort should be studied over a longer period of time.

Since the effort began, law enforcement officials have summoned 75 known members of four gangs into "call-in" sessions, where police warn them that any future violence will mean consequences for the entire group. Turnout was too low at the first two meetings, and police are considering whether to gather those groups again. A fifth session was held in the Downtown Denver Detention Center and targeted a variety of gang members just before their release.

Of the 75 attendees, at least 20 availed themselves of tattoo removal, job training and other services. Cooks said she worried there weren't enough services available to offenders.

"It seems like we're getting to the right population," said Paul Callanan, project manager for the Gang Reduction Initiative of Denver, which provides logistical support for Ceasefire. He said the success of the approach is the role it plays with the city's 23 other anti-gang strategies. "The mere fact these people are reaching out for help, I think that shows there's a bulk of gang members who want to get out."

The goal [of Ceasefire] was to send a message that the entire group will face scrutiny for the actions of one or two.

Six others who were called in have since been arrested. And just one of the four gangs has caused the kind of violence that police said warranted the law enforcement "intervention" that Ceasefire prescribes.

Is Pressure Effective?

Police said members of that gang were responsible for several incidents since its representatives were called in, including the Feb. 9 shooting of a man in the chest at West Arkansas Avenue and South Federal Boulevard, the March 13 shooting of another man in the 1400 block of North Zenobia Street, and a situation two days later in which they aimed a gun at a group of people on West Hillside Avenue. Detectives arrested two men in those cases.

As part of a Ceasefire response, officers arrested 19 members of that gang on a variety of offenses, such as outstanding warrants and probation violations. They made more than 60 probation and parole compliance checks. The goal was to send a message that the entire group will face scrutiny for the actions of one or two, Fleecs said.

Did it work?

"There's this feeling of pressure," said Cisco Gallardo, program director for Denver's Gang Rescue and Support Project, which is not affiliated with Ceasefire. "If that's what they wanted to happen, they definitely did that."

Still, Gallardo wondered if the pressure would last.

"For me, the jury is still out," he said. "There's a little pressure. At the same time, is it enough pressure?"

Fracturing Gangs Has Increased Violence in Chicago

Matthew Blake

Matthew Blake is a journalist who has worked at the Newberry Library and for such news outlets as In These Times, Daily Whale, Progress Illinois, Chicago Journal, *and other venues.*

Chicago Police Superintendent Garry McCarthy has pinned the 2012 rise in the city homicide rate on gangs. McCarthy asserts that gang members commit up to 80 percent of all Chicago murders and shootings, and that the fracturing of gangs has lead to an increase in violence. The police department has worked with not just City Hall on the problem, but also Cook County, the state of Illinois and the Obama administration on new measures to combat gangs.

But like overall city violence, gang violence is on a long-term decline despite the uptick this year. Moreover, there are changes in what constitutes a gang and how gangs use violence. Gangs are not just more splintered, their leadership is increasingly younger and more fluid.

The Changing Nature of Gangs

CPD [Chicago Police Department] defines a gang as "an organised group with a recognized leader whose activities are either criminal or, at the very least, threatening to the community." The definition makes it sound like gang members are readily apparent. "Gangs display their identity and unity in obvious ways such as jewelry, colored clothing, jargon, and signals."

As the police chief since last year, McCarthy has built on the work of his predecessors and placed identified gang members in the city's CLEARpath data system. McCarthy has won early praise for gathering intelligence on gangs. "I think that the police are doing an excellent job targeting and recognizing gangs," says Ald. Emma Mitts (34th).

Gang data does provide some unfavorable statistics about the Chicago area. There are estimated to be more gang members in Chicago than any other city, including New York and Los Angeles, and the FBI National Gang Intelligence Center finds that there are more gang members per capita in Illinois than any other state.

But police department knowledge of gangs is imprecise. According to the Chicago Crime Commission, a nonprofit that publishes a yearly overview on street gangs, CPD identified metropolitan area gang population as anywhere between 68,000 and 150,000 members in November 2011, out of the 9.8 million residents in the metropolitan region.

There is also a lack of clarity in saying that a shooting is gang related. It could mean a gang member shooting a non-gang member, shooting a rival gang member, or—increasingly—shooting a member of the same gang. Albert Lurigio, a psychology professor at Loyola University in Chicago who studies crime, says that the "changing nature of gangs" means more homicides stem from "minor conflicts like an insult or sign of disrespect" in small gangs with no clear hierarchy.

Disordered Hierarchy

Chicago gangs were organized better and prone to greater violence between the 1970s and early 1990s. The Chicago Crime Commission 2012 *Gang Book* finds that gangs such as the Black P Stone Nation and Black Gangster Disciples fought sustained gang "wars" during this time. Tio Hardiman, director of Cease Fire Illinois, a group that treats violence as a public health issue, refers to these bygone large gangs as "nations" with their own culture and identity. "Homicides were much greater when you had more nations," Hardiman says.

It is literally teenagers that have decided their block has become a gang over something as simple as a dispute over girls.

Since the early 1990s, the criminal justice system apprehended key gang leaders and prevented subsequent leaders from emerging. Federal investigators also started to apply the Racketeer Influenced and Corrupt Organizations (RICO) act in prosecutions involving street gangs. The RICO act had typically been used on the mob. "The use of federal RICO laws definitely paid off," Hardiman says. Also, the Illinois Department of Corrections and Federal Bureau of Prisons grew effective at preventing incarcerated gang leaders from providing orders while in jail.

The result is that more gangs today are closer to fly by night operations than organized criminal enterprises. "Different groups keep popping up with people just naming gangs after their block or a rap group," Hardiman says. Also, teenagers increasingly lead these gangs.

Shoshanah Yedhudah, a community organizer at the Southwest Youth Organizing Project, works with Chicago Public School [CPS] students in neighborhoods such as Chicago Lawn and Gage Park. Yedhudah estimates that 4 in 10 students she works with identify as gang members. "It is literally teenagers that have decided their block has become a gang over something as simple as a dispute over girls," Yedhudah says.

Yedhudah says that this has lead to an increase in violence, which is borne out by some citywide statistics. Shootings of CPS students were up 22 percent in the 2011–12 school year, though fatal shootings were down to 24 from 28 in 2010–11.

Tha Chicago Crime Commission Gang Book concludes that, "The disordered hierarchy implicates juveniles who are now increasing their criminal involvement and holding leadership positions within factions." This "makes the policing of gang activity progressively more complicated, since law enforcement cannot easily cripple the gang from the top down."

The City Reacts

While the city of Chicago has taken numerous steps to combat gang violence, initial efforts did not address gang splintering. In January [2012], CPD announced that the Englewood and Harrison police districts would work with the federal government to investigate gun-tracking cases. In June, after urging this spring from Chicago Mayor Rahm Emanuel, Gov. Pat Quinn signed into law a state RICO measure to target gangs as criminal organizations. These policies may prove effective, but they target gangs that operate as rational criminal enterprises.

The city has also responded to gang violence that stems from irrational, interpersonal conflict. In May, Emanuel announced that Ceasefire would get a grant from the Chicago Department of Health for their work in mediating potentially violent gang conflicts. Ceasefire mediators are largely former gang members. The organization previously feared coordination with the city could undermine their work. But Hardiman says that Ceasefire is in full cooperation with the city and CPD. "We are one," Hardiman says.

And in July, CPD started to work with Cook County jail to deny no-cash bonds for identified gangs members released on certain misdemeanor offenses. These suspects must now sit in jail for up to 48 hours instead of being immediately released. McCarthy has explained that the idea is to provide a "cooling off" period before a gang member gets back on the street.

Yehudah applauds the city for partnering with Ceasefire but says that "more is needed." Specifically, more could be done by CPS. The *Chicago Tribune* reported in June that the tentative new CPS budget, contingent on a contract with the Chicago Teachers Union, cuts money for mentoring and after school programs. It bears watching what money is available for these programs. "CPS always seems to find money for other priorities," Yehudah says, citing school turnarounds where the district fires the entire school staff.

CPS traditionally relies on federal and state monies for anti-violence initiatives. The Teen Outreach program run by Southwest Youth Organizing Project, for example, is funded by the state. Hardiman says it is unfair to lay the blame on CPS, and that gang violence should not be yet another issue put on the embattled school system. "It is not their problem," Hardiman says. "They are supposed to be educating kids."

Gang Violence in Los Angeles Has Decreased

Advancement Project

The Advancement Project is a California-based public policy change organization rooted in the civil rights movement. The group focuses especially on education and criminal justice issues.

Advancement Project, a public policy organization that issued a well-publicized roadmap in 2007 to reduce gang violence in Los Angeles, has released a new report demonstrating the significant gains made toward curbing violence, based on the roadmap's recommendations. In fact, efforts in Los Angeles have been so successful that other cities across the nation are working to adopt some of the strategies that have succeeded in Los Angeles. As the City of Los Angeles continues to transform its approach for resolving this gang epidemic, Advancement Project is calling for the City's next mayor to continue investing in programs and strategies that have dramatically decreased violence in Los Angeles.

Call to Action

In a report released today, "A Call to Action: Los Angeles' Quest to Achieve Community Safety," Advancement Project says a major test will be whether the next mayor supports the Los Angeles Police Department's continued transformation under its current leadership and makes the Office of Gang Reduction and Youth Development (GRYD) a permanent, independent institution with the political strength to tackle community conditions that lead to violence.

Advancement Project, "New Report Shows 'Marshall Plan' to Curb Gang Violence in L.A. Is a Success," advancementprojectca.org, November 26, 2012. Copyright © 2012 Advancement Project. All rights reserved. Reproduced by permission.

"Thanks to Mayor Villaraigosa, the LAPD, gang interventionists and many community partners, the City of Los Angeles has seen a dramatic decrease in violence, but there is still much left to do," said Connie Rice, co-director of Advancement Project. "The conditions that spawn gang violence remain largely unchanged in L.A.'s most vulnerable communities. Los Angeles cannot rest until every family enjoys the first of all civil rights—safety—and the first of all freedoms—freedom from violence. We must provide youth greater alternatives that pre-empt them from joining gangs, and we need the political will for a truly comprehensive solution with government-community partnerships at both the City and County level, tailored to yield results for each neighborhood."

Five years ago, Advancement Project issued "A Call to Action: The Case for Comprehensive Solutions to L.A.'s Gang Epidemic," a groundbreaking analysis and strategy that explained why Los Angeles' 30-year "war on gangs" had failed to quell either gangs or gang violence and provided a comprehensive series of recommendations for effectively improving safety and stopping the spread of gang violence. The current report assesses the progress L.A. has made and presents a vision for building on current gains to achieve greater public safely in the places where children still suffer chronic exposure to trauma and violence.

Since 2007, these new strategies have decreased gang violence by 15 percent, and in 2010 the homicide rate was at its lowest since the 1960s.

"'A Call to Action' offered concrete recommendations that laid the foundation for the City's Department of Gang Reduction and Youth Development," said Mayor Antonio Villaraigosa. "Our GRYD strategy has lead to significant decreases in violence in some of our most crime-ridden communities, demonstrating a breakthrough in gang-violence reduction and affirming the success of our holistic approach."

Since the release of a "Call to Action," in 2007, Advancement Project has worked closely with City officials to put these recommendations into place. Since then, the City has seen greater success in decreasing gang violence with gang-related crime reduced by over 15 percent and 35 percent fewer gang-related homicides surrounding neighborhoods served by the Mayor's GRYD Office and by Summer Night Lights, a summer violence reduction strategy.

"The recommendations in a 'Call to Action' were a catalyst for law enforcement to begin working with gang interventionists—a partnership that has helped Los Angeles turn around its gang epidemic," said Los Angeles Police Chief Charlie Beck. "This ongoing collaboration will be critical as we continue working to ensure that all of our city's neighborhoods enjoy safety and stability."

Reasons for the City's Success in Significantly Reducing Violence

- Catalyst to City's new approach to gang violence: Based on Advancement Project's recommendations to create a central entity that manages gang violence prevention in areas where the violence was concentrated, the City of L.A. created the GRYD Office to focus public resources where it is needed the most—on 12 gang violence hot zones identified in conjunction with community leaders. Since 2007, these new strategies have decreased gang violence by 15 percent, and in 2010 the homicide rate was at its lowest since the 1960s.

- Transformation of L.A. Police Department: The LAPD has transformed the way it deals with gangs, from an overbroad suppression strategy to relationship-based, problem-solving policing.

- Training gang interventionists: Advancement Project's Urban Peace Academy established the Urban Peace Academy to train gang interventionists, the only publicly funded training program in the nation for gang interventionists. The academy has trained more than 1,200 gang interventionists and more than 400 police officers to work together, which has resulted in collaboration and shared accountability to achieve public safety.

Despite these accomplishments, the City faces a number of ongoing challenges and opportunities for investment including:

- All sectors must work toward eliminating the root conditions in communities that perpetuate violence.

- Law enforcement reform must continue with a move toward community oriented, solutions-based policing model.

- Seize the opportunity presented by criminal justice realignment through AB 109 to reform the state's criminal justice system by shifting away from mass incarceration and foster rehabilitation in order to prevent recidivism and to facilitate a true reintegration of ex-offenders.

How to Return New York City to the Street Gangs

Heather Mac Donald

Heather Mac Donald is a John M. Olin Fellow of the Manhattan Institute and a contributing editor to New York's City Journal. *She is the author of several books, including* Are Cops Racist? *and* The Burden of Bad Ideas: How Modern Intellectuals Misshape Our Society.

Crime in New York City has dropped 80% since the early 1930s, a decline unmatched anywhere in the country. The change has yielded an explosion of commerce in once forlorn neighborhoods, a boom in tourism, and a sharp rise in property values. Nowhere were the effects more dramatic than in the city's poorest areas.

Proactive Policing

When the bullets stopped flying, entrepreneurs snapped up the vacant lots that had served as breeding grounds of crime. Senior citizens were able to visit friends without fear of getting mugged. Children could sleep in their own beds rather than in bathtubs, no longer needing shelter from stray gunfire. Target, Home Depot and other national chains moved into thoroughfares long ruled by drug gangs, providing jobs for local workers and giving residents retail choices taken for granted in middle-class neighborhoods.

Most significant, more than 10,000 black and Hispanic males avoided the premature death that would have been their fate had New York's homicide rate remained at its early-1990s

Heather Mac Donald, "How to Return New York City to the Street Gangs," *The Wall Street Journal*, August 11, 2013. Reprinted from *Wall Street Journal*, copyright © 2013 Dow Jones & Company. All rights reserved. Reproduced by permission.

apex. Blacks and Hispanics have made up 79% of the decline in homicide victims since 1993.

New York's previously unimaginable status as America's safest big city is now in jeopardy thanks to a rising campaign against its proactive style of policing. In 1994 the New York Police Department, led then by Commissioner William Bratton, embraced the revolutionary concept that the police could actually prevent crime, not just respond to it after the fact.

The department began analyzing victim reports daily to target resources to where crime patterns were emerging. Top brass held commanders accountable for the safety of their precincts. And officers were expected to intervene when they observed someone acting suspiciously—maybe asking the person a few questions, perhaps frisking him if legally justified. In so doing, they sent the message in violence-plagued areas that law and order was still in effect.

If the residents of the tony Upper East Side faced a similar risk of getting shot at recreational basketball games, the police would be out in force in that neighborhood.

Such proactive stops (or "stop-and-frisks") have averted countless crimes. But a chorus of critics, led by the New York Times, charges that the NYPD's policy is racist because the majority of those stopped are black and Hispanic. Every declared Democratic candidate for mayor in 2013 has vowed to eliminate stop-and-frisks or significantly reduce them. A federal judge overseeing a class-action lawsuit against the NYPD has already announced her conviction that the department's stop practices are unconstitutional, the prelude to putting the department under judicial control.

Demographics of Crime

Omitted from these critics' complaints is any recognition of the demographics of crime. Blacks were 62% of the city's murder victims in 2011, even though they are only 23% of the population. They also made up a disproportionate share of criminals, committing 80% of all shootings, nearly 70% of all robberies and 66% of all violent crime, according to crime reports filed with the NYPD by victims and witnesses, usually minorities themselves.

Whites, by contrast, committed a little over 1% of all shootings, less than 5% of all robberies, and 5% of all violent crime in 2011, even though they are 35% of New York City's population. Given where crime is happening, the police cannot target their resources where they're needed without producing racially disparate stops and arrests.

Critics also contend, among other charges, that the absolute number of stops—680,000—is too high and demonstrates illegality. But there were nearly 900,000 arrests and summons last year under the far more exacting standard at probable cause. It is not surprising that a police force of 35,000 witnessed 680,000 instances of reasonably suspicious behavior among New York's 8.5 million residents. If 25,000 officers in enforcement commands made just one stop a week, there would be over a million stops a year.

Violence continues to afflict minority communities. A rash of shootings during outdoor basketball games this summer should remind New Yorkers of what is at stake in the stop-and-frisk debate. The victims include a 4-year-old boy killed last month in the Bronx when two thugs started shooting at each other across a playground, and a 25-year-old member of the Harlem Youth Marines, an anti-gang group, killed during a shootout in June.

If the residents of the tony Upper East Side faced a similar risk of getting shot at recreational basketball games, the police would be out in force in that neighborhood, too, looking for the signs of gang activity and for individuals who appear to be carrying guns.

Increased Violence

Attacks on police officers have also skyrocketed this year. On Wednesday night, a thug on a bicycle shot the plainclothes officer who had just stopped him for suspicious behavior. This is the 10th time a cop has been shot in 2012, which is more than in the previous four years combined, reports the New York Daily News. Gun violence on the year is up 8.3% through Aug. 5, as stop-and-frisks dropped 34% between the first and second quarters of 2012, according to the New York Post.

It is too soon to tell whether the rhetorical campaign against the allegedly racist police is behind the onslaught against officers, or if the drop in stops has led to the rise in shootings. Over the long term, however, there is no doubt that getting rid of proactive policing will return New York to the bad old days of youth wolf packs and the flight of businesses and residents from the city.

No policing strategy is as effective in reducing violence as New York-style law enforcement. The cities offered up as alternative models by the NYPD's critics—such as Boston, Chicago and High Point, N.C.—have much higher rates of crime than New York.

The department should do everything it can to minimize the friction caused by its stop policy—above all by making sure that officers courteously explain to subjects they stop why they were approached. Being stopped if you are innocent of wrongdoing, even if the officer has legal grounds for doing so, is without question humiliating and maddening. But being shot when you are innocent of any wrongdoing is far worse.

New York's triumph over the lawlessness that was wasting lives and leading it to economic ruin is the greatest urban policy success of the last quarter-century. It proved that society has the capacity to reassert norms of civilized behavior even when they appear to have permanently broken down.

Putting that triumph at risk will take its greatest toll on the very individuals whom the NYPD's critics purport to speak for.

Santa Ana Violent Gang Crime Reported Down 40 Percent

Denisse Salazar

Denisse Salazar covers breaking news for the Orange County Register.

Santa Ana police officials say they have seen a near 40 percent decrease in violent gang crime so far this year and hope to keep gang killings at levels not seen in more than a decade.

In 2011, the city saw a 45 percent drop in gang-related homicides, the most significant reduction since 2006.

Now, with gang homicides nearly back to levels not seen since 2000 in a city that is home to some 5,000 documented gang members, top brass at the Santa Ana Police Department are being recognized for efforts to stamp out gang violence— historically a difficult task because of the reluctance of witnesses to step forward out of fear of retaliation.

Police Chief Paul M. Walters was presented with a Distinguished Service Award from the Orange County Gang Investigators Association for his department's success in fighting gang-related crime.

In an interview this week, Walters said it's special to be recognized by the association, which is made up of about 450 members from throughout Southern California and focuses on strengthening the investigative efforts against gangs.

"To me, it's particularly nice when you have the people that are really doing the work recognize you," Walters said.

When Walters was appointed chief of police in 1988, gang crime was exploding around the country.

"It was like this phenomenon that just swept across the United States," Walters said. "Even small cities were just having horrible gang crimes, and everybody was trying to respond to it and trying to figure out what to do."

To combat the growing gang violence, Walters formed Orange County's first and only Gang Homicide Unit and partnered closely with parole and probation officers, the District Attorney's Office and the FBI. Later, he hired an in-house firearms expert and formed a full-time SWAT team to deal with the most violent criminals.

Walters said the challenge is trying to keep evolving and adjusting crime-fighting techniques.

"It's everything you can throw at them, because otherwise they'll destroy your community and that's true no matter what city you go to," Walters said. "You shouldn't be afraid of your life and terrorized by gangsters."

Santa Ana—with a population of about 325,000—also has the most gangs, with nearly 100 identified.

Some gang-related homicides take months or years to solve because of the difficulty in getting witnesses to cooperate.

Gang homicide detectives investigated six murders in 2011. Four have been solved, officials said. There have been three gang-related murders so far this year. Two remain unsolved.

The unit solves 66 percent of the homicides investigated, which is above the FBI's national standard, said Sgt. Lorenzo Carrillo, who heads the department's gang investigative unit.

"Everyone we have in the Gang Homicide Unit has worked as a gang suppression officer (and has) focused on gangs as a patrol officer, so they have a long history with the gangsters and they are able to sit across the table and not only talk about what happened in that particular case but the history, the rivalries, the who's who," Carrillo said.

Witnesses Won't Cooperate

Some gang-related homicides take months or years to solve because of the difficulty in getting witnesses to cooperate.

"That is probably the biggest obstacle we have, to get cooperation from witnesses who live in the area due to fear of retaliation," said Cpl. Dave Rondou, who investigates gang homicides.

One case is telling.

It was Christmas night in 2005 when 25-year-old Pedro Cortes Teran was hanging out with friends in an alley behind the 2500 block of South Baker Street when two vehicles drove into the alley. Shots were fired from one of the vehicles and Teran was struck six times in the back and once in the chin.

The suspects fled. Teran was taken to Western Medical Center-Santa Ana, where he was pronounced dead.

Gang detectives spent about 12 hours going over the crime scene, finding witnesses, interviewing them and developing leads, but the case went cold.

About a year and half later, gang member Juan Avelar was arrested in connection with a domestic violence incident. A person involved in the incident confirmed Avelar was the shooter in the Christmas night killing.

Avelar was charged with murder in 2006 and was found guilty by a jury. He is currently serving a life term without the possibility of parole.

"In this case, we were able to build a rapport with people who were out there who normally are scared to come forward," Rondou said.

To help solve gang homicides, the Santa Ana P.D. launched a Gang Homicide Reward Program in May 2007. It's funded with a $1 million gift from an anonymous donor and so far, more than $250,000 has been paid out.

Gang Member Talks

Other times, Santa Ana detectives catch a break and gang members decide to cooperate and testify against their fellow gang members in exchange for their freedom.

A former Santa Ana gang member who requested anonymity because of safety concerns was the driver in three separate car-to-car shootings against rival gang members in the early 2000s. All of the shootings were fatal.

The 27-year-old joined his neighborhood gang when he was in middle school. He said he was seeking protection from gang members who harassed him every day on his way to and from school.

"At the time it was a no-brainer," he said. "They showed me love."

He was 17 years old when he went on his first "mission" to kill on sight any rival gang member.

"When you kill someone, your homies give you more respect," he said. "That's what I wanted at the time."

The gang member was eventually arrested for committing other gang-related crimes and was later linked to the three murders. He remembers sitting in jail and realizing he was going to spend 25 years to life in prison. He didn't want his son to grow up without a father.

"It was a big awakening for me, and obviously after that I said 'this isn't for me' and I started cooperating," he said.

He testified in three trials and spent four years in jail.

Thinking back to his gangster days and the crime-filled life he led, he said: "It's pretty much stupid. You are fighting for a street that's not yours. . . . It's a silly game."

Gang Violence Has Fallen in Aurora, Colorado

Brandon Johansson

Brandon Johansson is a staff writer for the Aurora Sentinel.

Covered from head to foot in tattoos, the man strolling through a gas station parking lot on East Colfax Avenue quickly caught the gang officers' eyes.

"Staying out of trouble?" Officer Doug Pearson asked as he held the man's hands over his head, frisking him.

"Yeah, yeah," the tattoo-covered ex-gangster nicknamed "Speedy" told him with a chuckle.

"Good to hear," Pearson said.

Building Relationships

Minus the frisking, badges and gang tattoos, the friendly chit-chat looked more like two neighbors catching up in their backyards than a meeting between cops and a hardened ex-gang member on Colfax.

That friendly approach is crucial to building relationships with the hundreds of gang members who Aurora police come in contact with, Pearson and his gang unit partner Officer Jeff Longnecker said.

"If there's not a rapport they'll just completely shut down and not give you any information whatsoever," Longnecker said.

And the approach seems to be working. The department last week released its annual gang report, which showed a steady drop in gang crime, particularly violent crime.

According to the report, violent gang crime was down slightly from 2011 to 2012, and is down more than 35 percent compared to annual averages between 2006 and 2011.

APD [Aurora Police Department] breaks down gang crime into two categories. One is gang-related crime. That can be anything from a gang member beating his girlfriend, to a gang member getting his car stolen.

The other is gang-motivated crime. Those are crimes police believe were committed to benefit the gang. It could be a gang member shooting a member of a rival gang, or property crime aimed at scoring cash for the gang.

Police logged just nine gang-motivated violent crimes in 2012, down from 29 the previous year. All nine of those were aggravated assaults, a steep drop from 2006, when there were 43 gang-motivated aggravated assaults.

For the third-consecutive year, there were no gang-motivated murders in Aurora, according to the report, though there were three gang-related murders.

Today's gang members have learned that being "flagged" by police as a gangster makes their life much tougher if they wind up in court.

Sgt. Mike Gaskill, who oversees the department's gang unit, said gang-motivated crime can be tough to track, and sometimes police don't know until well after a crime was committed whether it was gang motivated.

"Just because we can't prove at the time that it benefited the gang doesn't mean that it doesn't, it's just that we can't classify it at that time," he said.

Gaskill said today's gangsters are also less likely to admit their gang membership. Whereas gangsters were once proud of their allegiance, and often boasted about it to seemingly anyone who would listen, Gaskill said today's gang members have learned that being "flagged" by police as a gangster makes their life much tougher if they wind up in court.

"They might not be willing to admit they are a gang member, even though they are. Which makes it harder for us as law enforcement," he said.

Identifying Gang Members

For the officers in the unit, that means looking for the telltale signs of gang affiliation. Sometimes that means a style of dress, other times it means certain sports teams favored by a particular gang.

As they cruised down Montview Boulevard last week, the two officers stopped a man who at first looked like he might be affiliated with one of the Hispanic gangs known in the area—shaved head, plain white tank top, shorts that reach below the knee and socks pulled up high. One arm was covered in tattoos, and he had an Oakland Raiders jersey draped over his other.

But when they hopped out to chat with the man, they realized he wasn't a gang member, just a man out looking for work.

"Everybody thinks I am because of the tattoos," the man said when the officers were done. "But I just like tattoos."

After they sent the man on his way, Pearson said it's not uncommon for those street contacts to come up empty.

"When you look at the cover, it's not always the same as what's inside," Pearson said.

But those contacts do help the officers gather intelligence.

Last year, that keen understanding of the city's gang scene helped investigators nab a gang member who opened fire on an Aurora apartment complex with an assault rifle, narrowly missing a family in a minivan and peppering a 10-year-old boy with bullet fragments.

In that case, 23-year-old Awath Hammad, a Rollin' 60s Crip, was sentenced to more than 100 years in prison. Another man involved in the shooting, Malcom Henderson, a Stormin' 80s Blood, was sentenced to five years.

The two men bolted from the scene after the shooting, but gang officers tracked them down and arrested them within three days.

Longnecker said those arrests were particularly satisfying because the shootings marked one of those frustrating crimes where gang violence spills over to truly innocent people who aren't involved with gangs at all.

As for the city's gang crime on the whole, Gaskill said that while the numbers point to a decline, the problem remains steady and his officers don't have a problem staying busy seven days a week.

"Just like anything else in crime we have peaks and lows," he said.

CHAPTER 3

Do Antigang Policies Violate Civil Rights?

Chapter Preface

In November of 2013, police in Santa Barbara, California, made a concerted effort to confront gang violence. Gang activity had been on the increase throughout 2013, sparked by what Police Chief Cam Sanchez said was "a nexus between the Mexican Mafia and local gang activity."[1] In response, the city decided to initiate a large scale, dramatic push to arrest gang members. The program, called "Operation Falling Dawn," led to sixty-eight arrests and a dramatic press conference in which a wall was covered with mug shots of those captured. Sgt. Riley Harwood declared that the operation was the end of a new status quo of severe gang violence in the city. The new push against gangs was also to include a gang injunction that would make it easier to arrest gang members.

However, in January 2014, shortly before the gang injunction was to go into effect, a suit was filed against the Santa Barbara police department on behalf of six of the people whose mug shots were displayed at the Falling Dawn press conference. According to Kelsey Brugger, writing in the *Santa Barbara Independent*, the plaintiffs claimed that they were wrongly identified as being gang members and that the press conference libeled them and inflicted emotional distress. The lawyer for the plaintiffs, James Segall-Gutierrez, said, "These are people who are being affected in a very real way in terms of jobs and relationships."[2] Kat Swift, in a January 14, 2014, editorial in the *Independent*, argued that "Chief of Police Cam

1. Quoted in Lara Cooper, "Santa Barbara Police Cracking Down on Gangs with 'Operation Falling Dawn,'" Noozhawk, November 20, 2013. http://www.noozhawk.com /article/police_chief_touts_68_gang_arrests_in_city-wide_crackdown_20131120.

2. Quoted in Kelsey Brugger, "Operation Falling Dawn Defendents File Slander Claims Against City, Police," *Santa Barbara Independent*, January 17, 2014. http://www .independent.com/news/2014/jan/17/operation-falling-dawn-defendants-file-slander -cla/?print.

Sanchez is not above defaming others in order to advance his political career. At least a couple of individuals he has claimed were 'gang members' were, in fact, housewives without any prior arrest records."[3]

The lawsuit asked for more than $1 million in damages per client. The city could also apologize and drop the effort to pass a gang injunction. While the police believed that the injunction was necessary to reduce violence, the plaintiffs felt it would enable police to arrest and harass innocent people.

The viewpoints in the following chapter examine other arguments over the relationship between gang prevention and civil rights, particularly in such areas as profiling, prison conditions, and street stops.

3. Kat Swift, "SBPD Gang Hysteria," *Santa Barbara Independent*, January 14, 2014. http://www.independent.com/news/2014/jan/14/sbpd-gang-hysteria/?print.

Antigang Strategies Justify Profiling and Discrimination

Robert J. Durán

Robert J. Durán is associate professor of criminal justice at New Mexico State University.

I'm driving through the 'hood of Ogden [Utah] one evening and notice two undercover police vehicles stopped with their lights flashing. A friend and I park and walk over to the scene with my video camera. I've been recording police stops for two years as part of a local community group pushing for police accountability called POP. As I get closer to where the two white plainclothes officers are standing, I notice they are talking with three young Latino males in an apartment complex parking lot. Such a profile of officers and suspects equals the Gang Unit. As I begin recording the scene, a red undercover police car pulls up behind me and begins observing our actions. The three Latino youth look young standing in front of the larger adults. Police lights spin in the darkness while spotlights shine on the scene. Shortly after my arrival, several sheriff's vehicles pull up and the officers exit and begin observing the area. There are now nine officers present. The two cops begin taking pictures of the youth, who appear to be only 13, 14, and 16. Toward the end of the stop, the three youth appear to be joking with the officers as they are patted down and questioned. After some time goes by they are released.

A middle-aged Latina comes out from the apartment complex frustrated and begins yelling at the officers to quit harassing her nephew. She says, "You should be chasing the real

Robert J. Durán, *Gang Life in Two Cities: An Insider's Journey*, New York: Columbia University Press, 2013, pp. 40–49. Copyright © 2013 Columbia University Press. All rights reserved. Reproduced by permission.

criminals, not my nephew. Quit harassing my family or I will press charges." The white gang officer responds, "We didn't pull over anyone, Ma'am, who is your family?" She responds, "The one over there. Don't be judging a book by its cover. He works. He has a license. He is in no gang." The gang officer responds, "We stopped the vehicle for a traffic violation. No one is harassing, Ma'am. He didn't even receive a traffic violation." The Latina responds, "You told him that if he didn't cooperate you would take him to jail. Get the real fucking criminals." The gang officer quickly challenges the comment: "What was that, Ma'am? What did you say?" The aunt's male companion encourages her in Spanish to remain calm. The officer looks towards me and states, "Did you get that [video-record of the woman swearing]? Probably not, you are just after the cops." I respond calmly, "I'm capturing everything." As the police officers leave the scene I give the woman a business card and contact information for POP. She repeats, "This ain't right," but she seems unsure of how to stop the police from doing whatever they want. Individuals that I interview tell me that filing a complaint is a waste of time because it goes nowhere or results in only enhanced police harassment. The pattern of Latino and black submissive compliance with a high number of police stops and questioning is continually repeated in Denver and Ogden. Individuals who are stopped hope for the chance to be released without an incident. Some individuals are not so lucky and are led away in handcuffs or are demeaned, brutalized, or occasionally killed.

The Rise of Gang Enforcement

The early 1980s in Denver and early 1990s in Ogden can be seen as a period of early formation of gang enforcement as an institutional framework for responding to actual and perceived gang activity. This was not the first time authority figures targeted gangs, . . . but it was the first time in which gang enforcement became federally funded and organized around a gang suppression model involving intelligence gathering, aggressive law enforcement, and prosecutorial interest. In the post-civil rights era, such a strategy to suppress gangs ensured that the level of cultural activism never again achieved the momentum that was attained in the 1960s and 1970s. Law enforcement took the lead as the authorities began identifying who gang members were and what they were perceived to be doing.

A large number of cities since the mid-1980s have created specialized gang units to support a "war on gangs" that will eliminate this alleged threat.

The concept of gangs began to legitimize and open the door to more aggressive forms of law enforcement. Violating an individual's civil rights became less of a concern as barrios and ghettos began to be equated with breeding grounds for gangs and criminality—the two terms were used interchangeably. Gangs were characterized as nonwhite and then were argued to be more criminal. Gang labeling is important for at least three reasons: (1) it is overly broad in definition but specific in terms of whom the label is applied to; (2) it allows for selective and aggressive enforcement; and (3) it responds to groups formed from racial oppression with neutral-sounding code words that perpetuate a cycle of increased oppression.

In response to this image of a gang member as a new "urban predator," a large number of cities since the mid-1980s have created specialized gang units to support a "war on gangs" that will eliminate this alleged threat. Through a survey of 261 police departments, [M.W.] Klein (1995) found that intelligence gathering, crime investigation, and suppression were the most common police actions against gangs, and that many states had instituted increased consequences for gang-related crimes. [I.A.] Spergel (1995) agreed that a vigorous "lock-'em-up" approach remained the key action of police departments, particularly in large cities with acknowledged gang problems. Police officers routinely recognize how such a war on gangs is hindered by traditional constitutional protections but have developed support to create methods and tactics to sidestep disapproval; in essence they have become legitimated. Diaz (2009) argued that the federal government became involved in gang suppression after the 1992 Los Angeles riots. The Safe Streets Initiative allowed for joint federal, state, and local agencies to participate in combating gangs. The Department of Justice continued this pursuit to bring down gangs by merging organized crime statutes under federal racketeering laws (Racketeer Influenced and Corrupt Organizations Act, or RICO) that required making street gangs, which primarily lacked a leader hierarchy and military structure, fit their needs. These ongoing efforts have institutionalized the war on gangs by targeting immigrants and social groups that are deemed a threat to national security.

Police officers had a full range of reasons to initiate and later justify a "criminal" stop when speaking with barrio residents.

Understanding the impact of the criminal justice system on the lives of gang members and the communities they live in was a significant part of my research because it was constantly mentioned and observed as a problem. The substantial impact of criminalization on barrio communities is all the more amazing when one realizes that many gang researchers have failed to explore what role the executive branch of government plays in altering life chances. This [viewpoint] seeks to correct this omission in the scholarly literature by highlighting law enforcement's role in the definition of the situation by labeling gang behavior as primarily involving people of color. The chapter introduces the argument of contemporary racialized oppression, defined as the actions and motivations of the state to utilize the stratification of racial and ethnic group hierarchies in the United States to exercise power in a cruel and unjust manner for the purpose of maintaining colonialism.

Legitimated Profiling

In both Denver and Ogden, police officers were primarily deployed in high-crime districts. These were more often neighborhoods with a higher concentration of Latinos and blacks (50–90 percent) and economic poverty (20–70 percent). The police departments' diversity paled in comparison to these neighborhoods. Approximately 20 percent of Denver police officers and 5 percent of Ogden police officers were Latino. Since most street crime did not occur in plain sight, police officers had to determine which people were engaging in criminal activity.

The police focused on making stops based on the legal justification of reasonable suspicion and probable cause. Probable cause includes a belief, based on objective facts, that supports the suspicion that a person is committing or about to commit a crime. A lead prosecutor in northern Utah described reasonable suspicion as "facts and circumstances that would lead a reasonable officer to believe that there is a particular problem or indication of criminal activity." Together, reasonable suspicion and probable cause legitimated a wide-ranging assortment of stops.

However, this led to a confrontational relationship between police and many residents in Denver's and Ogden's barrios because residents often believed that police officers were using gang and criminal stereotypes to predicate stops. Most of my respondents reported that they had been stopped for a variety of reasons that were not criminally predicated; in other words, they were profiled. Latino youth reported that common reasons the police gave for the stop included, "It looked like I was wearing 'gang' clothing" (i.e., clothing from sports teams and hip hop clothing), "I was assumed to be out too late," "People matched my description," "There were reports of shots fired," "We had more than three people in the car," or "We looked suspicious." Other community members were stopped because of minor traffic violations that could be detected only with strict scrutiny. If there were no traffic violations, police officers had the option of using vehicle safety ordinances, such as lacking a front license plate, violating noise ordinances, having overly tinted windows (Utah), hanging rosaries or objects from the rear-view mirror (Colorado), standing or driving around in a known gang area, or driving a customized (i.e., lowrider) vehicle. In sum, police officers had a full range of reasons to initiate and later justify a "criminal" stop when speaking with barrio residents.

Reasonable Suspicion

The wide array of justifications created confusion on the part of Latino and black youth. D-loc, a 25-year-old ex-gang member from Denver, described a meeting between community members and police officers. He attempted to learn more about the legal term "reasonable suspicion":

> We were really trying to have some meaningful conversation with 'em and say, "why you pull us over, because there are four of us in a car?" [Police response:] "Agh, reasonable suspicion." "What if we were just walking down a street?" "Agh, reasonable suspicion." "Well how come you stop our little brothers and sisters on the street, they ain't doing nothing." "Agh, reasonable suspicion." It could be anything. We started getting upset because every answer they gave us was reasonable suspicion. So I said, "What's reasonable suspicion?" They said, "There could have been a crime in your community and the description they gave might fit the description of someone walking down the street. There was a robbery that happened in a house and the suspect was described as a possible Hispanic male between 5'6" and 5'9", ugh, between 120 lbs and 170 lbs." "Shit, that's almost every male in my

community between those ages and that description. That's half of the population in my neighborhood. So that gives you any reason to stop any one of us and be a bunch of assholes to anybody walking down the street because you feel like it?"

D-loc stated that he started attending police presentations about gangs to critique their phony criteria of gang identifiers. To the police, everything in terms of urban style was considered to be affiliated with gangs, from how your shoes are tied, to hats and how they are worn, to how you sit, to every imaginable symbol or article of clothing. D-loc argued that most of the time this has nothing to do with gangs but is just the style of youth fitting in with their peers.

They [the police] stopped me for everything. They even stopped me a couple times to tell me they liked my car.

POP observations supported Latino and black claims of harassment. During their five years of watching the police in Denver, Randolph and Pam, two middle-aged white police-observers reported the countless times they witnessed Gang Unit officers searching suspected gang members' vehicles for drugs and weapons. Pam reported that officers would stop young men for unclear reasons and take them all out of the vehicle. Randolph said the officers would then ask everyone in the car for identification, check them for outstanding warrants, search their pockets, and then send them on their way. He explained:

So that happens over and over again, and it's the same general age group, ethnic group, gender group that it happens to time and time again, and no one is arrested. Like detention and searches are supposed to be based on a reasonable suspicion that a crime has been or is about to be committed, so what is the crime here? It seems that being a Chicano youth for the Denver Gang Unit is reasonable suspicion of criminal activity. . . . So a lot of times, what we see is the Gang Unit rides around using bogus traffic violations as an excuse to stop any car that has more than one young man of color. It can either be black or Chicano, or even Asian sometimes. A little-known fact is that whites get in gangs too, but they never get stopped.

Pam and Randolph thought that maybe if Latino youth began dressing in suits they wouldn't be stopped by the police for meeting a profile, but they wondered how unusual that would be to stop the harassment. They both argued that the police net was long and broad in its application to youth of color.

Stopped for Everything

Traffic violations were highly discretionary and also very difficult to prove or disprove. Several researchers have attempted to determine the role and significance of this practice as racial profiling and how it is used to further an investigation into the identity of occupants and search for possible contraband. In November 2000 Denver initiated a task force to assess racial profiling in the city by requiring officers to fill out contact cards. The study found that from June 1, 2001, to May 31, 2003, the number of stops experienced by each racial and ethnic group was similar to their numbers in the city population, but that Latinos and blacks were searched at two to four times the rate of whites.

Based on POP observations, the city of Ogden utilized racially profiling far more than Denver, possibly owing to the lack of organized community resistance. Chicle, a 26-year-old ex-gang associate from Ogden, said, "They would make up reasons for maybe going too fast or going too slow, or maybe you were swerving. I've been pulled over fifteen to twenty times and I haven't gotten a ticket." Although happy to not receive a ticket, Chicle believed a legitimate stop by the police entailed a consequence, whereas a fictitious reason included being released. Cola, a 27-year-old ex-gang member from

Ogden, recalled, "They stopped me for everything. They even stopped me a couple times to tell me they liked my car. I'm not sure what that had to do with anything. At the time I thought it was nothing, but now that I think back, I realize they would take down all of our names. We were just glad that we weren't in trouble for anything." Cola recalled purchasing low-profile tires for one of his vehicles that resulted in a higher than average number of stops, but such selective enforcement appeared odd when large trucks driven by white cowboys did not result in similar treatment.

A large number of researchers have reported police harassment within Latino communities.

The observed and described police discretion produced an elusive standard for establishing reasonable suspicion and probable cause because it was highly influenced by extralegal factors (e.g., age, class, gender, neighborhood, and race). [E.] Anderson (1990) found that police officers become "willing parties" to "color-coding" that entails making race, age, class, and gender presuppositions as to who commits crime and who will be perceived as dangerous. While researching as a member of POP, I found Gang Unit stops were particularly influenced by age, gender, race, and local gang stereotypes in 100 percent of the forty-seven observed police stops. In Ogden it was observed that when dispatch reported Hispanic males involved in an incident, the Gang Unit was more likely to accept the call to investigate. The rationale for many of these stops and subsequent detentions appeared far-reaching. Compliance with picture taking and information resulted in release from custody. The rationale of gang officers would leave researchers believing that most people stopped were gang members. However, gang members in both cities were a small percentage of barrio youth. The average number of youth who join gangs continues to be very low. Even in Los Angeles, the gang capital of the world, it is estimated that only 4 to 14 percent of youth join gangs. According to the data I accumulated over five years, there were definitely a greater number of associates than actual members of the gang—probably a 20-to-80 ratio.

Barrio youth faced greater difficulty entering different parts of the city because law enforcement often associated this behavior with causing problems with rival gangs. Randolph, the POP member from Denver, described a situation in which a car was stopped:

> And the officer will say, "I recognized the people in the back seat of that car as being from East Denver and I wanted to know why they were in West Denver." Now that's not a reasonable suspicion of a crime. People in the United States are supposed to have freedom of movement. . . . Obviously the reason they were there was because they were cruising during Cinco de Mayo. . . . It's a famous event for a lot of youth and so they will go cruise Federal [Boulevard] because it's a big thing. So it's a ridiculous reason to say someone is from another jurisdiction and that's why I stopped them.

Ethnicity, Age, Gender

Pam and Randolph described how, along with several additional groups from the community, they became involved in observing police stops during Cinco de Mayo. They reported that the number of tickets or citations decreased from 2,500 in 1996 to 15 in 1998. The police observers provided a presence to document that many of the citations given were not illegal and the reasons for the stops were also fabricated.

According to the Gallup Poll as cited in the *Sourcebook of Criminal Justice Statistics*, Latinos (63 percent) report a greater belief that racial profiling is widespread in motorist stops on roads and highways than whites (50 percent). Latino youth in the barrio believed they were stopped simply because of their profile, and most had witnessed experiences where their white friends were treated more leniently. A large number of researchers have reported police harassment within Latino communities. [D.] Bayley and [H.] Mendelsohn (1968) reported: "The police seem to play a role in the life of minority people out of all proportion to the role they play in the lives of the Dominant majority [whites]."

A large number of residents believed that police were there to enforce social control over the neighborhood and the people who lived there.

A third demographic factor community members believed they were stopped for was their gender. Men or teenage boys were perceived as more highly targeted than women or teenage girls. Thus the women interviewed described fewer negative interactions with the police than the men, but they believed that the police would try to use them to gather information. The young women who attended ASAP thought the men were stopped and harassed more by the police. Randolph, the POP member in Denver, commented on this pattern: "If it's a car full of girls, they are far less likely, we saw, to be stopped. So, like, for every car full of girls they stopped, they stopped ten cars full of guys and we know that multiple passengers were much more likely to be targeted." If ascribed characteristics were not enough for police to profile individuals as gang members, many Latino youth matched the criteria by their clothes, haircuts, numbers, or tattoos (interviews with Denver and Ogden Gang Units and gang protocol). Most youth dressed in clothes that were fashionable with their peers. This created great confusion for the police, and even for gang members, when the majority of youth dressed in baggy clothes from urban hip-hop brands . . . and clothing with numbers. . . . [M.] Fine et al. (2003) reported that urban youth in general felt disrespected by police, and that adults in positions of authority often equated youths' urban clothing as a symbol of their criminal inclination. Lucita, a 25-year-old gang associate from Ogden, recalled seeing the police approach her Mexican American friends: "They get harassed, they get questioned, they get pulled over for any reason because they wear their pants a certain way, which is funny because you catch these white kids trying to do the same thing but they never get asked those questions. They never get asked 'Why you dress like that?' or 'Where are you going?'"

Latino youth who dressed similarly to others in their neighborhood increased their differential treatment by both authority figures and peers. Urban attire brought the possibility of negative treatment by authority figures but also approval from peers. Whites, on the other hand, were more likely to escape negative gang connotations being associated with their identity.

With gang officers making a high percentage of their stops based on extralegal factors related to age, gender, neighborhood, race, and gang stereotypes, community members were skeptical about police officers' stated primary objective as targeting crime. Rather, a large number of residents believed that police were there to enforce social control over the neighborhood and the people who lived there. Police officers often faced difficulty legitimizing their actions with the people they were policing. The profiling increased conflict, but individual officers lacked the structural power to alter where they were deployed and how they prevented crime. Their structural vulnerability led officers to dismiss claims of racial profiling. Nevertheless, the everyday motions of police work legitimated a focus on extralegal factors.

Police in Chicago Do Not Discourage Gangs but Act Like a Gang Themselves

Ta-Nehisi Coates

Ta-Nehisi Coates is a national correspondent for The Atlantic, *where he writes about culture, politics, and social issues. He is the author of the memoir* The Beautiful Struggle.

I spent last week trooping through North Lawndale, on the West Side of Chicago, with the *Atlantic*'s video team. We spent much of Friday with some positive folks over at the Better Boys Foundation (BBF) in K-Town. Then we went outside to get some sense of the neighborhood. I've spent a lot of time in North Lawndale over the past year. It is one of the roughest neighborhoods in Chicago. It is also achingly beautiful. Wide boulevards cut through the neighborhood, the old Sears building looms in the distance, and the great greystones mark many of the blocks. If you stand at the corner of Springfield and Ogden, as I have, right next to the Lawndale Christian Health Center across from Lou Malnati's Pizzeria, you can see the great wealth of Chicago, indeed the great wealth of America, looming over all those who long toiled to make it so.

The Police and Violence

That Friday, it snowed all day and we walked the blocks, Sam, Kasia, Paul and me, with our guides, running mostly on the odd joy one imbibes from the kind of exploration that should be what journalism is about. Towards the end of the afternoon we were standing on a corner shooting one of our hosts. Kids were walking home. We were standing on a street designated as a route for Chicago's Safe Passage program [to protect students going to and from school]. Volunteers, bundled like scientists of the arctic, stood across the way, nodding as children passed.

The afternoon was quiet. The street-lights were just beginning to flirt. There was no sun. A group of older boys, with no books, came aimlessly down the street. Our host called one of them over and hassled him for not having stopped by BBF recently. BBF is a fortress in a section of this long warred upon section of the city. Kids can go to BBF to read, make beats, make video or play table-top hockey. The conversation between our host and the kid was familiar to me. It was the way men addressed me, as a child, when they were trying to save my life. Aimlessness is the direct path to oblivion for black boys. Occupy the child till somewhere around 25, till he passes out of his hot years, and you may see him actually become something.

Catercorner to the volunteers of Safe Passage, two cops sat in an SUV, snug and warm. Our video team was shooting the conversation between our host and the kid. One of the cops rolled down his window and yelled, "Excuse me you need to take your cameras off this corner. It's Safe Passage."

I didn't know anything about Safe Passage and the law. If the program prohibits video footage on a public street, I haven't been able to document any record of it. But it is police, after all, which is to say humans empowered by the state with the right to mete out violence as he sees fit. We backed up a bit. Our host kept talking. The cops yelled out again. "You need to move, bud. This is Safe Passage." At this point our host yelled back and contentious back and forth began. Things calmed down when one of our cameramen walked down the street with our host to get a few different shots.

Jon Burge and Chicago Justice

A few months ago, on one of my other trips to Chicago, I was at a dinner with a group of wonks. The wonks were upset that the community, and its appointed representatives, would not support mandatory minimums for gun charges. I—shamefully I now think—agreed with them. It's not simply that I now think I was wrong, it's that I forgot my role. I mean no disrespect to my hosts. But whenever reformers convene for a nice dinner and good wine, a writer should never allow himself to get too comfortable.

Police address us with aggression, and their default setting is escalation. De-escalation is for black civilians.

One of my friends, who grew up on the South Side, and was the only other black male at the table, was the only one who disagreed. His distrust of the justice system was too high.

Perhaps this is why:

> During his more than 30 years behind bars, Stanley Wrice insisted he was innocent, that Chicago police had beat him until he confessed to a rape he didn't commit. On Wednesday, he walked out of an Illinois prison a free man, thanks to a judge's order that served as a reminder that one of the darkest chapters in the city's history is far from over....
>
> Wrice, who was sentenced to 100 years behind bars for a 1982 sexual assault, is among more than two dozen inmates—most of them black men—who have alleged they were tortured by officers under the command of disgraced former Chicago police Lt. Jon Burge in a scandal that gave the nation's third-largest city a reputation as haven for rogue cops and helped lead to the clearing of Illinois' death row. Some of the prisoners have been freed; some are still behind bars, hoping to get the kind of hearing that Wrice got that eventually led to his freedom.

The scandal of Jon Burge, which will trouble Chicago police for many years to come, is the worst of something many black folks feel when interacting with police in any city. Police address us with aggression, and their default setting is escalation. De-escalation is for black civilians.

When the officer wanted us to move, there was a very easy way to handle the situation. You step out your car. You introduce yourself. You ask questions about what we're doing. If we are breaking the law, you ask us to move. If we are not breaking the law and simply making your life hard, we are likely to move anyway. You are the power.

Holding Down the Corner

The cop did not speak to us as though he were human. He spoke to us like a gangster, like he was protecting his block. He was solving no crime. He was protecting no lives. He was holding down his corner. He didn't even bother with a change of uniform. An occupied SUV, parked at an intersection, announces its masters intentions.

It was only a second day there, and our first real one out on the street. It only took that short period to run into trouble. I was worried about the expensive equipment. But it was the conventions of community that protected us. People would walk up and ask us what we were doing. I would tell them we were shooting the neighborhood, or had just finished interviewing some elder—Mr. Ross, Mrs. Witherspoon—and they would smile. "So Mr. Ross is famous, huh?"

No such social lubricant exists for the police. If you are young and black and live in North Lawndale, if you live in Harlem, if you live in any place where people with power think young black boys aren't being stopped and frisked enough, then what happened to us is not a single stand-out incident. It is who the police are. Indeed they are likely a good deal worse.

What people who have never lived in these neighborhoods must get, is that, like the crooks, killers, and gangs, the police are another violent force that must be negotiated and dealt with. But unlike the gangs, the violence of the police is the violence of the state, and thus unaccountable to North Lawndale. That people who represent North Lawndale laugh at the idea of handing over more tools of incarceration to law enforcement is unsurprising.

As we were finishing up, the officer who yelled at us got out the car and asked for the driver of our vehicle. It wasn't me.

"I happened to notice your sticker is expired," the officer said, handing a ticket to Kasia.

"It's a rental," she replied.

"Well give it to them," he told her walking away. "They'll know what to do with it."

The cop got back in his heated car. On the other corner, Safe Passage stood there, awaiting children, huddling in the cold.

Racial Profiling Targets Innocent Children

Courtney Bowie

Courtney Bowie is a senior staff attorney with the ACLU Racial Justice Program. She focuses on litigating cases related to the "school-to-prison pipeline." Prior to joining the ACLU, Bowie was an attorney with the Southern Poverty Law Center, where she directed the work of its Mississippi Youth Justice Project and litigated systemic claims on behalf of students with disabilities in Alabama, Mississippi, and Louisiana.

On December 16, 2010, West High School officials in Salt Lake City, Utah invited the Metro Gang Task Force into the school to conduct a gang sweep. Students identified, searched and interrogated by the police were mostly Latino/a or, in the case of Kaleb Winston, African-American. He was targeted by his school and by the Task Force as a potential gang member, searched and accused of being a tagger. As an artist, Kaleb had a notebook full of drawings in a backpack manufactured to look like it had been spray-painted. But because graffiti is loosely defined, if at all, the police decided Kaleb was a "gang tagger" despite his denials. Kaleb was then forced to hold up a sign with the words "My name is Kaleb Winston and I am a gang tagger." Law enforcement officers told him that this information was being placed into a database and that the information would be removed if he did not get into trouble for two years. Kaleb was emotionally devastated by the experience. He is not and has never been in a gang. Yet, his attendance at school that day, not bad behavior, made him the subject of intense police scrutiny and he now lives with the fear that the police view him as a suspect.

Courtney Bowie, "Wearing a Hoodie While Brown Does Not Mean You Are In a Gang," ACLU online, December 13, 2012. Copyright © 2012 American Civil Liberties Union. All rights reserved. Reproduced by permission.

Targeting Students by Race

Today [December 13, 2012], the ACLU Racial Justice Program and the ACLU of Utah filed suit against the Salt Lake City School District, the Salt Lake City Police, and the police departments responsible for the Metro Gang Task Force to vindicate the rights of all the students caught up in the December 2010 gang sweep. Because of the district's vague gang policies and the racial profiling that follows, the sweep ended with children being photographed and placed into a gang database accessible to law enforcement throughout the country. The majority of these students, including Kaleb, have never committed a crime other than attending school in brown skin.

Going to school in a hooded sweatshirt is common for teenagers throughout the country. However, students of color run the risk of being racially profiled by their teachers and the police for their apparel choices simply because they are not white. Anti-gang policies have led to gang databases filled with the names and pictures of students of color who have not been convicted of any crimes, but have been victimized by police or school racial profiling. The result in Salt Lake City, Minneapolis, Minnesota, Orange County and Los Angeles, CA and a number of other cities, is that children are stuck in these criminal databases indefinitely; this is what happened to Kaleb Winston as a freshman at Salt Lake City's West High School.

Suspects Rather than Students

Like the case of Trayvon Martin [a seventeen-year-old African American shot and killed in 2012 by neighborhood watch volunteer George Zimmerman], where a young, brown child in a hooded sweatshirt was racially profiled and a horrible tragedy followed, we should all be outraged. In that case, an individual gunned down a young man who looked suspicious to him because he was: walking, wearing a hoodie and cloaked in brown skin. Here the outrage should be because parents entrusted their children to the school district and the school district suspected them of being gang members. The result? The police placed their pictures in a gang database for some indefinite period of time despite the fact that none were arrested for a crime. As a result of this racial profiling by their teachers and police, those students' lives are changed forever. Labeling them falsely as gang members unfairly stigmatizes them in the eyes of others. More importantly, assuming that they are gang members solely because of their race or ethnicity changes their view of themselves and their role in society. It is particularly tragic because this police and school conduct does not deter gang activity. Instead, it only discourages students of color from seeing the schoolhouse as a place of learning and it reminds them that they were born to be suspects rather than students.

In Prison, Gang Affiliation Is Used as an Excuse for Inhumane Treatment

Amnesty International

Amnesty International is an international human rights organization.

More than 3,000 prisoners in California are held in high security isolation units known as Security Housing Units (SHUs), where they are confined for at least 22 and a half hours a day in single or double cells, with no work or meaningful rehabilitation programs or group activities of any kind. Over 1,000 are held in the SHU at Pelican Bay State Prison, a remote facility where most prisoners are confined alone in cells which have no windows to the outside or direct access to natural light. SHU prisoners are isolated both within prison and from meaningful contact with the outside world: contact with correctional staff is kept to a minimum, and consultations with medical, mental health and other staff routinely take place behind barriers; all visits, including family and legal visits, are also non-contact, with prisoners separated from their visitors behind a glass screen.

Isolation in the Name of Gangs

Under California regulations, the SHU is intended for prisoners whose conduct endangers the safety of others or the security of the institution. Around a third of the current population are serving fixed SHU terms of SHU confinement (ranging from a few months to several years) after being found guilty through the internal disciplinary system of specific of-

USA—The Edge of Endurance: Prison Conditions in California's Security Housing Units, *Amnesty International,* September 2012, pp. 2–3, 42–44. Copyright © 2012 Amnesty International. All rights reserved. Reproduced by permission.

fences while in custody. However, more than 2,000 prisoners are serving "indeterminate" (indefinite) SHU terms because they have been "validated" by the prison authorities as members or associates of prison gangs. According to figures provided by the California Department of Corrections and Rehabilitation (CDCR) in 2011, more than 500 prisoners serving indeterminate SHU terms had spent ten or more years in the Pelican Bay SHU; of this number, more than 200 had spent over 15 years in the SHU and 78 more than 20 years. Many had been in the SHU since it opened in 1989, held in conditions of extreme isolation and environmental deprivation.

No other US state is believed to have held so many prisoners for such long periods in indefinite isolation. The main route out at the SHU for prisoners with alleged gang connections has been to "debrief", a process requiring them to provide information on other gang members which many decline to undertake because of the threat of retaliation. Although prisoners may also be released from the SHU if they have been "inactive" as a gang member or associate for six years, many prisoners have been held long beyond this period. Until now, these prisoners have had no means of leaving the SHU through their own positive behaviour or through participating in programs. Many prisoners have spent decades in isolation despite reportedly being free of any serious rule violations and—if they are serving a "term to life" sentence—without any means of earning parole. Prisoner advocates and others have criticized the gang validation process as unreliable and lacking adequate safeguards, allowing prisoners to be consigned to indefinite isolation without evidence of any specific illegal activity, or on the basis of tenuous gang associations, on evidence often provided by anonymous informants.

In March 2012, the CDCR put forward proposals which, for the first time, would provide a "step-down program" (SDP) for prisoners serving indeterminate SHU terms, using what the department has called a "behaviour-based model" to enable them to earn their way back to the general prison population. Amnesty International welcomes in principle plans to provide a route out of isolation through prisoners' own behaviour. However, the SDP—which would take place in four stages, each lasting a minimum of one-year—does not allow any group interaction for at least the first two years. No changes to the physical conditions of confinement are proposed for the Pelican Bay SHU, where prisoners would spend at least two years in the same isolated conditions of cellular confinement as they are now. Prisoners could still be held in indefinite isolation if they fail to meet the criteria for the SDP. In continuing to confine prisoners in prolonged isolation—albeit with shorter minimum terms than under the present system—California would still fall short of international law and standards for humane treatment and the prohibition of torture and other ill-treatment.

As some other states have shown, cutting down on "supermax" confinement has released resources for alternative strategies to improve prisoner behaviour, including gang diversion programs.

Amnesty International does not seek to minimize the challenges faced by prison administrators in dealing with prison gangs and individuals who are a threat to institutional security and recognizes that it may sometimes be necessary to segregate prisoners for disciplinary or security purposes. However, all measures must be consistent with states' obligation under international law and standards to treat all prisoners humanely. In recognition of the negative effects of such treatment, international and regional human rights bodies and experts have called on states to limit their use of solitary confinement, so that it is imposed only in exceptional circumstances for as short a period as possible. As described below, Amnesty International considers that the conditions of isolation and other deprivations imposed on prisoners in California's SHU units breach international standards on humane treatment. The cumulative effects of such conditions, particularly when imposed for prolonged or indefinite periods, and the severe environmental deprivation in Pelican Bay SHU, in particular, amounts to cruel, inhuman or degrading treatment, in violation of international law.

Reforms Needed

Amnesty International's recommendations to the California authorities, developed in more detail at the end of the report, include:

- Limiting the use of isolation in a SHU or similar environment so that it is imposed only as a last resort in the case of prisoners whose behaviour constitutes a severe and ongoing threat to the safety of others or the security of the institution.

- Improving conditions for all prisoners held in SHUs, including better exercise provision and an opportunity for more human contact for prisoners, even at the most restrictive custody levels.

- Allowing SHU prisoners to make regular phone calls to their families.

- Reducing the length of the Step down Program and providing meaningful access to programs where prisoners have an opportunity for some group contact and interaction with others at an earlier stage.

- Immediate removal from isolation of prisoners who have already spent years in the SHU under an indeterminate assignment.

In making these recommendations, Amnesty International is aware that CDCR has faced a number of challenges in recent years, including cuts to its budget for rehabilitation pro-grams. However, as its own figures show, the SHUs cost sig-nificantly more to run than general prison population facilities, despite providing the barest minimum amenities for those confined in them. As some other states have shown, cut-ting down on "supermax" confinement has released resources for alternative strategies to improve prisoner behaviour, in-cluding gang diversion programs. . . .

More Safeguards Needed

"People are validated on the basis of one individual saying 'I heard him say something' . . . or 'I saw him do something.' There is no policing of the system, they do whatever they want and they get away with it. The SHU units are like torture chambers . . . my main issue is with the solitary confinement and the vali-dation." Sister of a 50 year old gang validated prisoner, origi-nally sentenced to 15 years to life; he has now been impris-oned for 25 years and has been in solitary confinement for a total of 21 years.

SHU terms in California are subject to administrative review, but there is no external review of such assign-ments other than through the courts.

Amnesty International was unable to obtain a detailed break-down of the current California SHU population; how-ever, based on the overall figures on numbers in the SHU, it appears that around a third are serving determinate (fixed) SHU terms for serious offences or rule violations set out un-der Title 15 of the California Code of Regulations, Section 3315. Guidelines for the length of fixed SHU terms range from two months to five years for offences including sexual misconduct, harassment, threats, assaults, escape attempts, weapons possession and murder (Section 3341.5). Some of the offences carrying a SHU term include acts which are classified as serious assaults or other offences but may also be symptoms of behavioural or mental health problems. Offences listed as serious rule violations (SRV) carrying a potential SHU term also include offences such as "Tattooing or possession of tattoo paraphernalia", "Self mutilation or attempted suicide for the purpose of manipulation" and "A repeated pattern of rule violations for the same offense".

Prisoners charged with serious disciplinary offences are entitled to some due process protections in the internal proceedings against them, although these are less than those required in a criminal trial. They include written notice of the charges and a statement of the evidence to be relied on, a hearing before an impartial officer at which the prisoner may produce documents in his or her defence and has a conditional right to call and question witnesses. The accused prisoner will also be assigned a staff member to assist in the investigation and/or preparation and presentation of a defence, where this is considered necessary for a fair hearing. Prisoners accused of criminal misconduct while in prison may also have their cases referred to the prosecutor for trial in the criminal courts which could result in an additional prison sentence within the range set for the criminal offence. Once a prisoner has been found guilty of an offence carrying a possible SHU term, the Institutional Classification Committee (ICC) decides on whether or not the prisoner will be assigned to the SHU and sets the term according to the guidelines for that offence. Prisoners serving determinate SHU terms can have their terms reduced for good behaviour. The term may be extended if the prisoner commits repeat offences while in the SHU, or they may be retained in the SHU if their release is considered to constitute a severe security risk.

The large majority of the California SHU population— some 2,280 prisoners—have been assigned to indeterminate (indefinite) SHU terms on the basis of being "validated" as a member or associate of a prison gang. Validations are made through an internal procedure and prisoners can be assigned to indefinite SHU terms by CDCR without being accused or convicted of any offence or rule violation.

In his 2011 report on solitary confinement, the UN Special Rapporteur on Torture and other cruel, inhuman or degrading treatment or punishment urged states to adopt procedural safeguards when imposing solitary confinement, in order to reduce the chances of it being applied in an "arbitrary or excessive" manner. His recommendations included providing individuals with a "genuine opportunity to challenge both the nature of their confinement and its underlying justification through a process of administrative review"; informing the detained person of what he or she must do to be removed from solitary confinement; a meaningful appeals process and review by an independent body, as well as an opportunity to appeal to the courts.

SHU terms in California are subject to administrative review, but there is no external review of such assignments other than through the courts. As described below, prisoner advocates and others have criticised the internal review process as failing to provide adequate safeguards, particularly for prisoners given indefinite SHU terms on the basis of a gang validation. While prisoners may bring court actions challenging their gang validations or SHU assignments or conditions, prison administrators are afforded wide discretion in measures taken on security grounds and prisoners face significant obstacles in bringing such actions.

Inhumane Treatment

"My position remains . . . California Department of Corrections/ PBSP-SHU policies and practices have violated our human rights and subjected us to torture—for the purpose of coercing inmates into becoming informants against other inmates, etc., for the state." Letter written to Amnesty International by prisoner held in solitary confinement in Pelican Bay SHU.

As noted above, for prisoners who are validated as gang members or associates, the main route out of the SHU to date has been to "debrief", a process which requires them to renounce their gang connections and provide detailed information on other alleged prison gang members or associates. This is a procedure which many prisoners decline to undertake for various reasons: they may not want to "snitch" on (inform on) other inmates on principle or because of the risk of retaliation against themselves or family members; in other cases prisoners dispute being involved in a gang or they dispute the level of their alleged involvement or deny any recent involvement, and thus maintain they have no evidence to provide. In 2005, CDCR introduced new regulations to provide an alterative route out of the SHU by creating a category of "inactive status", whereby SHU prisoners who can establish they have not been involved in gang activity for a minimum of six years may be considered for release from the SHU by the classification committee.

Many prisoners have . . . complained that, despite being free of any gang activities or association for six years or more, they have not been held eligibly for release from the SHU.

Despite the introduction of "inactive" status, hundreds of prisoners have continued to serve years of indefinite SHU confinement. In August 2011, CDCR spokesperson Scott Kernan reported that the average term served by prisoners in SHU housing was 6.8 years. However, as described above, more than 500 prisoners in Pelican Bay in 2011 (around half the prison's SHU population) had spent over ten years in the SHU; 222 had been in the SHU for 15 or more years and 78 more than 20 years. Many had been in Pelican Bay SHU since it opened in 1989, all held under the same harsh conditions throughout that period, without any ability to change their situation through good behaviour or programming. Amnesty International has received information about prisoners, some now in their late 50s or 60s, who have spent decades in the SHU without incurring any significant disciplinary write-ups; for some prisoners, their first major "rule violation" was for participating in the 2011 hunger strike [protesting prison conditions].

Concerns About Gang Validation Criteria

"So, the suffering is to make you feel hopeless, helpless . . . and your only way to stop the suffering is to debrief." Gang validated inmate currently held in Pelican Bay SHU.

Amnesty International is not in a position to evaluate in detail the criteria deployed in the gang validation process. However, there has been widespread criticism from prisoners, advocates and others that the present process is too discretionary and that, while three independent "source items" are required to validate someone as a gang member or associate, these need not relate to any specific gang-related activity or illegal act. The independent "source items" can include tattoos or being in possession of books or materials or, it is alleged, simply being seen talking to another alleged gang member in a unit where a prisoner is housed. If a prisoner is visited by someone suspected of being a gang member or associate, even if they are visiting as a relative, this can also be used against them. Information may also be based on confidential sources which can be impossible to challenge.

Under the regulations, the term "associate" is someone deemed to be involved "periodically or regularly with members or associates of a gang", and, it is alleged, can be loosely applied to include association with prisoners of similar background and the same racial group. Many prisoners have also complained that, despite being free of any gang activities or association for six years or more, they have not been held eligibly for release from the SHU. Prisoners have allegedly been denied inactive status based solely on being on a list of names provided by anonymous informants, or for having certain drawings in their cell or being in possession of literature associated with political ideologies such as the Black Panthers [a black revolutionary socialist organization].

The harsh conditions of the SHU have presented prisoners with what a federal court has described as "an overwhelming incentive for an inmate to embrace the risk of debriefing". According to prisoner advocates and attorneys, pressure to debrief can serve to compound problems regarding the reliability of evidence. As one lawyer put it, if a prisoner is wrongly assigned to the SHU, or has no current information, but decides to debrief, "they won't have evidence to disclose, so they have a strong motive . . . to name others/anyone". He referred to this as a "downward spiral" in which the named individuals will in turn be placed in the SHU, as can anyone associating with them.

Police Use Criminal Profiling to Fight Gangs and Crime

Sunil Dutta

Sunil Dutta is a Los Angeles Police Department lieutenant and a patrol watch commander at the Foothill Division.

I was accused of racial profiling on the first traffic stop I made as a rookie LAPD officer in 1998. I had spotted a reckless driver speeding through the streets of Van Nuys in a large pickup truck, so I flipped on my lights and took up the chase. The driver eventually pulled over, but as I walked up to his car, he began shouting at me, accusing me of having stopped him because he was black.

Ethnicity and Crime Data

I could not sleep that night. A liberal academic before becoming a police officer, I had joined the Los Angeles Police Department hoping to make a difference. Yet here I was, on my first traffic stop, being accused of racism.

I thought of that incident again last week, when the LAPD was accused yet again of not adequately guarding against racial profiling by its officers. This time, it was the Department of Justice making the claim. As evidence, the agency cited a recording of two officers seemingly endorsing the practice in a conversation with a supervisor. One of the men said that he "couldn't do [his] job without racially profiling."

Racial profiling has consistently been one of the most confounding, divisive and controversial issues the police department confronts. A perception that police target members of specific ethnic or racial groups creates a deep divide between the police and the communities we serve. But as an officer who has spent a lot of time patrolling the city's streets, I just don't think the perception is accurate.

True racial profiling, in which people are targeted solely because of race or ethnicity, is both illegal and immoral. It destroys public trust and reduces the effectiveness of the police. There is no place for it in law enforcement. And I firmly believe that most LAPD officers support that viewpoint. Even the reported statement of the officer that he couldn't do his job without racial profiling was most likely misinterpreted.

Consider the gang officer in Foothill Division, where I work. Each day, they go out in the field looking for Latino males of a certain age who dress in a particular way, have certain tattoos on their bodies and live in an area where street gangs flourish. Does that mean they are engaging in racial profiling? No. They are using crime data to identify possible suspects. Ethnicity is just one of many criteria they consider.

The perceptions of some Angelenos are still rooted in memories of a time when minority members were frequently abused and ill-treated by police officers.

We have to acknowledge that there is a place for race and ethnicity in police work. If officers get information that a 6-foot-tall Asian man with a Fu Manchu mustache committed a robbery, they are of course going to target their search to tall Asian men with Fu Manchu mustaches. If the suspect is an 80-year-old white woman, the search won't focus on young black men. Officers are trained to use all the data available to them in apprehending criminals. When officers follow leads and stop people, they do use profiling, but it is profiling based on all actionable intelligence, which includes race as one of many criteria. I suspect the officer whose comment was caught on tape was talking about this kind of criminal profiling.

I am not naive enough to believe that pure racial profiling has never happened. In a department as large as ours, there may be isolated officers who haven't gotten the message. It's true that no officer in the department has been found guilty of racial profiling, but that is a difficult charge to substantiate. But in my experience, Los Angeles police officers are much less likely than the general public to act on personal prejudices and biases. We work in an ethnically diverse department and in ethnically diverse communities, and officers who aren't comfortable with that diversity aren't going to make it in police work.

Video to Build Trust

The LAPD has come a long way and has made concerted efforts to transform itself into a community-policing-based agency. But the perceptions of some Angelenos are still rooted in memories of a time when minority members were frequently abused and ill-treated by police officers.

For more than a decade, there has been a push to put video cameras in all patrol cars to record officer interactions with those they stop. There have been technical difficulties and problems with cost. But ultimately this is a crucial step to take to reduce community perceptions of racial profiling. We should also equip officers with personal video cams. Recording every police-citizen interaction would not only keep officers professional, it would greatly increase the conviction rate of criminals, reduce expenses of the criminal justice system and build trust in police-public relations.

The majority of hardworking and professional officers would benefit tremendously. All the false allegations made against them could be instantly dismissed, and complaint investigations would be much quicker and less costly. Additionally, the criminal justice system would save on investigative costs when a video recording demonstrated clearly that officers had a probable cause and obtained evidence properly. This could lead to more criminals pleading guilty, saving us long and costly court proceedings.

Many savvy officers have already started using cop-cams, purchasing them with their own funds. These officers realize the protection video recordings provide against false complaints. It is time for the department to institutionalize video recordings.

Police Balance Public Safety and Civil Rights in San Juan

Jacqueline Armendariz

Jacqueline Armendariz covers law enforcement, courts, and general assignments for The Monitor *in McAllen, Texas.*

The often delicate balance between civil liberties and law enforcement's goal of public safety is playing out in San Juan [Texas].

The target in between: gang members.

Checkpoints

For more than a year now, San Juan Police Chief Juan Gonzalez said his department has conducted checkpoints at certain locations in direct response to crimes investigators believe are gang-related. The criminal element—such as the Texas Chicano Brotherhood that rivals the older Tri-City Bombers gang, the Po'Boys and the Vallucos—has long plagued the Pharr, San Juan and Alamo area.

At a San Juan checkpoint, most cars attempting to pass through are stopped. Passengers are questioned and, in certain instances, individuals are asked by investigators to voluntarily submit to having photographs taken of their gang-affiliated tattoos. The information is then vetted for inclusion in a state database.

The chief describes the checkpoints as a "non-conventional, but legal investigative approach" that amounts to only a small portion of a larger initiative to curtail gang activity.

"We're not targeting any innocent people here," he said.

Still, organizations like the South Texas Civil Rights Project [STCRP], based in Alamo, have questioned whether the enforcement activity could potentially be a violation of the Fourth Amendment that keeps people free from unreasonable search and seizure.

"That certainly raises that alarm that what they're doing could be unconstitutional," STCRP lawyer Joseph Martin said. "Police have always been pressing against restrictions the Constitution puts on protecting rights of individuals."

"We Know What We're Looking For"

In Texas, police are prohibited from conducting roadblocks to check for drivers under the influence. However, city police sometimes perform checks for insurance, seatbelts and driver's licenses in places like Corpus Christi, for example.

In San Juan, the purpose of the checkpoints is two-fold: checking for those types of violations and gathering intelligence to enter into the state's GangScope database.

San Juan police, along with Hidalgo County Precinct 2 constables and narcotics K-9s, set up their operation following a drive-by shooting near the intersection of Seventh Street and King Road during a Thursday night in October this year.

Known gang members are targeted for immediate arrest if they are found to be in violation of any traffic laws.

A few cars in, at 3rd Street and Maldonado Drive, a man self-identified as a member of "*La Eme*," the notorious Mexican Mafia prison gang, police said. Officers on site asked him to remove his shirt so they could take photos of his tattoos.

"We know what we're looking for," Gonzalez said. "We know what colors they wear. We know their behavior. We even know the vehicles."

He said known gang members are targeted for immediate arrest if they are found to be in violation of any traffic laws, with the exception of speeding and an open container.

Police went out again in December on a Friday night to an area where they believe a family was shot at by gang members in October. They set up in the parking lot of Sorensen Elementary on Sam Houston Blvd.

Nearby residents gathered, curious as to what was going on.

Ray Reyes, who lives directly across from Sorensen Elementary, said officers told them it was driver's license checkpoint, but hadn't mentioned they were targeting gang members.

"This is kind of not normal; all these cops, especially like undercover and then to have the mobile command center," Reyes said, adding he appreciated the police presence, but would like them to respond to calls more quickly.

Is It Legal?

The San Juan police chief said he invited the STCRP to discuss concerns about the checkpoints this month after they filed an open records request.

STCRP lawyer Joe Martin said police enforcement activity often pushes against civil rights, calling it "a constant pressure people need to be aware of."

On face value, he said he doubted the constitutionality of the checkpoints and photographing people for inclusion in the GangScope database. He also said the STCRP encourages anyone affected by these checkpoints to contact the organization.

"There's basic constitutional issues involved, obviously the Fourth Amendment," he said.

Martin said a checkpoint with the purpose of detecting criminal activity is unconstitutional, problematic in the case of the gang checkpoints because they focus on gang membership.

Additionally, it can be a slippery slope that leads to profiling, particularly based on race, he said. A member of the public is often hard pressed to deny the request of a police officer, even if inclusion in the database is voluntary, he added.

"On the base of it, it seems highly questionable on whether this kind of checkpoint is constitutional," Martin said.

He could not be reached for further comment about STCRP's meeting with the San Juan police chief by press time.

Still, the San Juan police chief is adamant the checkpoints fall within the parameters of the law.

"They're limited. They're not infringement upon anything," he said. "We cannot do general checkpoints."

Gonzalez said the initiative has been evaluated by the city's legal department and police take steps to plan the checkpoints well in advance using their own intelligence.

He said anyone stopped also has the right to refuse being photographed. Though, in general, he said gang members are willing to self-identify.

"I can tell you 99 percent of the people we stop, they actually tell us they're with whatever gang," Gonzalez said.

He explained it's a lengthy process to submit data to Gang-Scope; officers corroborate claims and individuals must meet certain qualifiers. Once in the database, the information stays for a period of three to five years depending on further gang activity, he said.

The chief said he hasn't received any complaints from average citizens nor requests for removal from the database.

Though at first he said the checkpoints were done monthly, he said the actual tally over the past year and a half is just two or three operations that have averaged 8 to 10 arrests.

"It's a good thing that we're doing in the PSJA area, especially there in San Juan, because we've got a lot of gang activity," the chief said.

CHAPTER 4

What Is the Gang Problem Like in Other Countries?

Chapter Preface

Organized crime gangs, called the *yakuza*, are an established and influential part of Japanese society. The yakuza's roots may go back as far as the seventeenth century. Currently they number more than one hundred thousand members, dwarfing any organized crime group in the United States. They have political links to Japan's far right wing and are involved in legitimate and quasi-legitimate corporate business, as well as in criminal enterprises, according to Anthony Bruno in an article at crimelibrary.com.[1]

The yakuza's semi-legitimate status was underlined following the 1995 Kobe earthquake in Japan, when they were "one of the most responsive forces on the ground getting supplies to the affected areas."[2] The yakuza were also active following the massive tsunami of March 2011, sending "twenty-five four-ton trucks filled with paper diapers, instant ramen, batteries, flashlights, drinks," and other supplies to the hard-hit Tohoku region the day after the disaster.[3]

In his article on The Daily Beast website, Jake Adelstein noted that this is consistent with the yakuza's traditional image; they are often seen as peacekeepers, damping down street crime. One poll of adults under forty in Japan found that fully 10 percent of the respondents felt that the yakuza were "a necessary evil"—not a sentiment you would likely find about US gangs.

However, despite their occasional good works, the yakuza remain criminals, and dangerous ones at that. In 2012, the United States froze the assets of two major yakuza leaders be-

1. Anthony Bruno, "The Yakuza," crimelibrary.com, accessed February 15, 2014. http://www.crimelibrary.com/gangsters_outlaws/gang/yakuza/4.html.

2. Jake Adelstein, "Yakuza to the Rescue," The Daily Beast, March 18, 2011. http://www.thedailybeast.com/articles/2011/03/18/japanese-yakuza-aid-earthquake-relief-efforts.html.

3. Ibid.

cause of their involvement in "weapons trafficking, prostitution, human trafficking, drug trafficking and money laundering,"[4] according to a 2012 article by Justin McCurry in *The Guardian*.

Yakuza gangs are also responsible for violence within Japan. A war between two gangs, the Dojin-kai and the Kyushu Seido-kei, finally ended in 2013 after seven years, fourteen deaths, and a number of shootings and bombings. Some civilians were shot, and the proliferation of grenades became so prevalent that the Fukuoka Prefecture Police began distributing cash rewards for reports of grenades.

The viewpoints in the following chapter look at gang activity in countries other than the United States, including Mexico, Canada, Indonesia, China, and Russia.

4. Justin McCurry, "US Steps Up Offensive Against Japan's Yakuza Gangs," *The Guardian*, February 24, 2012. http://www.theguardian.com/world/2012/feb/24/united-states -offensive-japan-yakuza.

Crime in Mexico: Out of Sight, Not Out of Mind

The Economist

The Economist *is a British weekly news and business magazine.*

A human hellhole lies under the noses of American tourists driving from California into Mexico. Below the bridge leading into Tijuana is a dry canal strewn with heroin syringes that is home to countless migrants and vagrants, most of them thrown out of the United States for not having the right papers. Jesús Alberto Capella, Tijuana's chief of police, says their numbers have included about 10,000 ex-convicts turfed out of American jails this year. They live under tarpaulins and in foxholes dug into the side of the canal. The place is a cauldron of violence. It is also a focal point for President Enrique Peña Nieto's strategy of applying what officials call "social acupuncture" to some of the most dangerous parts of Mexico.

Struggling with Gang Violence

Felipe Calderón, Mr Peña's predecessor, made fighting organised crime the centrepiece of his presidency. Backed by the Mérida Initiative, a $1.9 billion American aid scheme that has supplied Black Hawk helicopters and X-ray machines to detect narcotics, Mexico's police, army and navy sought to dismantle drug mobs by capturing their bosses. But violence soared, at least 60,000 died, mostly in vicious turf battles between rival gangs.

Troubled by the bloody image this gave Mexico, Mr Peña has adopted a new approach since taking over in December. Its most eye-catching element is to pour 118 billion pesos

($9.1 billion) into the 220 most violent neighbourhoods in the country (some are in Tijuana), offering more schooling, jobs, parks and cultural activities to stop them becoming "crime factories". Footballers have joined in, providing soccer camps to slum kids who might otherwise want to become hired guns.

These are not new ideas. Efforts to mend the torn social fabric in the most crime-ridden cities, like Tijuana and Ciudad Juárez, started under Mr Calderón. Mr Peña has given them greater impetus, yet even his government recognises that they will not yield a quick pay-off. Meanwhile, it is under pressure to produce a coherent law-enforcement plan in a country where, according even to official statistics, almost nine out of ten crimes go unreported. Policing is a particular concern. "They are still in reactive mode. If there is a plan to go after drug-traffickers, it's being kept super-secret," says Vanda Felbab-Brown a crime analyst at the Brookings Institution in Washington.

> [The Mexican government's] claim to have cut the number of murders is at least partially offset by a 35% rise in kidnappings in the first eight months of the year, compared with the same period in 2012, as well as a surge in extortion, according to police statistics.

Officials say they have chalked up at least three tangible successes so far. The first is a decline in murders. According to police figures, these fell by 18% in the first eight months of this year. Second, the security forces have started to dismantle the Zetas drug gang that terrorised Mexico for years. In July the authorities arrested its boss, Miguel Ángel Treviño Morales. Mercifully, his capture did not lead to the sort of bloodletting that followed the arrest of drug kingpins in the past.

Third, the government has tried to impose a clearer chain of command by turning the interior ministry into the mother ship of Mexico's myriad federal security agencies. This involves swallowing Mr Calderón's once-omnipotent ministry of public security and also handling tricky public-order and civil-defence issues such as a teachers' strike and hurricane relief. Officials say the unified security apparatus makes it easier to co-ordinate anti-drug efforts with the attorney-general's office, the armed forces and state governments. Crime experts, however, blanch at the administrative nightmare the government has imposed on itself.

Limited Success

To many, the most tangible success of Mr Peña's government has been getting violence off the front pages of national and international newspapers. But its claim to have cut the number of murders is at least partially offset by a 35% rise in kidnappings in the first eight months of the year, compared with the same period in 2012, as well as a surge in extortion, according to police statistics. And these may vastly understate the problem.

According to estimates by INEGI, the national statistics institute, last year saw 105,682 kidnappings; only 1,317 were reported to the police. There were around 6m cases of extortion; the police put the number at 7,272. Using its own figures, Security, Justice and Peace, an anti-crime charity, says Mexico is currently the worst place for kidnapping in the world, and that more victims are being killed. It says Mr Peña lacks an anti-kidnapping policy and is downplaying the entire crime problem.

Other analysts agree that the government has yet to do anything to improve the quality of the police, end their culture of impunity and create courts with the guts and expertise to convict criminals. It is leaving much of the job to state governors, meaning the results will be patchy at best.

For months, officials have hummed and hawed over how to honour Mr Peña's campaign pledge to create a new federal gendarmerie. This was originally envisaged as turning 40,000 former soldiers into police to patrol troubled rural areas. Political infighting has reduced this promising idea to a shadow. Officials say the new force will now be only 5,000 strong. In line with the "social acupuncture" approach it will offer haircuts and dentistry as well as security. The resulting vacuum has been filled in parts of Mexico's poorer south by paramilitary self-defence groups, some in the pay of *narcos* and others set up to protect their communities from them.

A Coat of Paint

In such circumstances, some experts scoff at Mr Peña's "soft" approach to crime prevention. They want more petty criminals behind bars before they become murderers and kidnappers. Mr Capella, who has helped knock Tijuana's police force into better shape, says Mexico needs strong policing to halt the violence as well as social workers who pick up the pieces.

Under the Tijuana border crossing, that may mean sending in police to clean up the area, but also setting up booths to meet people expelled from the United States, offering them papers, psychological support, anti-drug counselling, food and shelter before they become a crime risk. With luck, the sleazy canal may even get a lick of paint, which would do wonders for many Americans' first impression of Mexico. Whether this is enough to make the country safe is another matter.

Canadian Gangs Are Linked to the Global Drug War

Jerry Langton

Jerry Langton is the author of Gangland: The Rise of the Mexican Cartels from El Paso to Vancouver; Showdown: How the Outlaws, Hells Angels and Cops Fought for Control of the Streets; *and* Fallen Angel: The Unlikely Rise of Walter Stadnick in the Canadian Hells Angels.

It was an arrest this week [March 2013] in Greece that put Canada's gang violence into perspective. The capture of Canadian Rabih "Robbie" Alkhalil in Athens for a first-degree murder in Toronto represents another enlightening piece of the puzzle that is Canada's role in the global war against organized crime.

Organized Crime Murders

To understand how it all fits together, it pays to revisit a bright, sunny day in June 2012. Toronto's Little Italy was alive with soccer fans who'd crowded the area's restaurants and cafés to watch a European Cup game. At the Sicilian Sidewalk Café at the corner of College and Montrose, the patio out front was packed. But there was one guy who didn't have a problem finding a seat.

Johnny Raposo was the leader of the McCormick Boys, and commanded respect in his community. As he was sitting out front enjoying the Sicilian's renowned gelato, he was approached by two road workers—who in Toronto in the summer are as commonplace and unremarkable as flies. Suddenly, the two men opened fire on the crowded patio. They knew what they were doing. Raposo died on the scene. Another man was badly injured. No other people on the crowded patio were hurt.

It was also a bright sunny day in Kelowna, B.C., in August 2011. Jonathan Bacon was pulling his Porsche Cayenne SUV out of the Delta Grand Okanagan Resort & Conference Centre when a Ford Explorer blocked his way. Four masked gunmen jumped out and filled the Porsche full of holes. Bacon died on the scene, another man was critically injured, a young woman was paralyzed from the neck down and two other passengers were mildly injured.

These two murders—ten months and more than 4,000 km [kilometers] apart—are two examples that illustrate how organized crime is fomenting violence in Canada.

Raposo was a drug dealer. The McCormick boys were a small but influential street gang with about 10 members and maybe two dozen associates they could count on. Like many street gangs in Canada, they took their name from a park they used to hang out in as teenagers—McCormick Park in Toronto's west end that is overlapped by Little Italy and Little Portugal.

[Dean] Wiwichar was a bad dude who had made his way through the Canadian corrections system.

Though few in number, the McCormick Boys wielded great authority because their drugs came directly from the Italian Mafia. They had graduated from street dealers to middlemen who moved product from the Mafia to other street-level dealers, including Hispanic and black gangs, in west Toronto. Although he was not known to be related to Luis "Chopper" Raposo, who was one of the Bandidos killed in the April 2006 Shedden Massacre, the two likely knew each other through shared connections with the Loners motorcycle gang.

Bacon was also a drug dealer. He was heavily involved with, said to be the co-leader of, the Red Scorpions. A multi-ethnic gang based in the rapidly growing Fraser Valley communities, the Red Scorpions began in a youth detention centre by a pair of Southeast Asian kids convicted of murder who sought mutual protection and, later, a source of income from drug sales. Like many other B.C. gangs, violent men (often white, like Bacon) worked their way to the top.

The two were not just similar, they were connected; allies in a global crime war.

A Web of Gangs and Violence

Raposo was allegedly killed by Dean Wiwichar and Alkhalil. Wiwichar was a bad dude who had made his way through the Canadian corrections system. Suspended from high school for fighting, he had been arrested several times for robberies and assaults, often employing masks and weapons.

When he hit 18 in 2005, he was given a 10-year sentence. At his March 2009 parole hearing, the decision-makers heard that while in prison he had been caught with weapons 10 times and had been involved in five assaults. They paroled him anyway. A month later, he was in a car wreck in Maple Ridge, B.C., that broke his leg. The driver was a fellow parolee and the car was leased by a fugitive. Since the police found a loaded handgun and marijuana in the car, Wiwichar went back behind bars. Inside, he continued his aggressive ways, even assaulting a guard with the walker he was issued to help with his broken leg.

After his next release, Wiwichar was arrested again in May 2012 and charged with 37 counts of firearms offenses. His co-accused were a woman named Juanita Hyslop and an alleged gangster named Philip Ley. Ley is alleged to be a member of the Red Scorpions (Bacon's gang) and is also alleged to have been the target of a failed assassination attempt orchestrated by the Dhak gang, which is also alleged to have been behind Bacon's murder.

Alkhalil has had a similarly checkered past. With two of his brothers already dead due to their involvement in gangs, Alkhalil appeared undeterred. In November 2012, he was one of several people arrested in Montreal in an operation police allege moved 75 kg [kilograms] of cocaine per week. At the scene, police confiscated 400 firearms, explosives, $255,000 in cash, marijuana, cocaine and other drugs. Among those arrested was the man police allege is the ring leader, Larry Amero. Not only is Amero well known as a high-ranking member of the Hells Angels, but he was also the man critically injured in the assault that killed Bacon.

According to police, Wiwichar and Alkhalil were working under the orders of Nicola "Nick" Nero (arrested at his Niagara Falls home) and Martino Caputo (arrested in Germany). Both men are alleged to have close ties to the Mafia and the Hells Angels.

The men who are alleged to have killed Bacon—Jujhar "Gianni" Singh Khun-khun, Jason Thomas McBride and Michael Hunter Jones—have ties to the Dhaks and also to their associated gang, the Duhres, and another gang, the Red Scorpions' archrivals, the United Nations.

Many of those gangs get their drugs not from the Mafia, but from sources in East Asia. It's also not a coincidence that the method Bacon's killers used originated in Colombia and is commonly used in Mexico, the places where cocaine distribution has led to sophisticated, incredibly bloody wars. All of the crime organizations that operate in Canada have some direct or indirect connections to the cartels there.

The consensus among law enforcement is that Raposo and Bacon were on the same side of the great organized crime divide, but killed for different reasons.

A Global Drug War

Raposo's was disciplinary. He worked as a middle manager for the Mafia/Hells Angels drug organization, but was eliminated when his gambling problem put him in so much debt with the suppliers that they felt they had no choice but to get rid of him. It's not just a code; it's a lesson to other employees.

Bacon, however, was a casualty of war. Long a very visible representative of his side, he was taken out by the other side. The motive might have been revenge for recent killings of Dhak/Duhre/United Nations associates, or it might have been because his plotting with Amero of the Hells Angels and James Raich of the closely associated (and inaccurately named) Independent Soldiers would have given his organization and allies the upper hand in British Columbia. Odds are it was both.

But it's misleading to say that Bacon was a victim of a Canadian gang war. It's more accurate to say that he was killed on the Canadian front in a global drug war that involves all the heavy hitters from Italy, China, the U.S., Latin America and everywhere else drugs originate or make their stop on their way to Canadian streets.

Medellín, Columbia, Fights Ongoing Drug Gang Violence

Toby Muse

Toby Muse is a journalist who writes for The Guardian, *a British newspaper.*

A team of bodyguards fans out through the three-storey building in central Medellín, calling out "clear" after each room is checked. One gunman remains stationed on each floor; another three guard the building's entrance.

New Drug Wars

With the area secured, a young man in a designer T-shirt and baseball cap emerges on to the roof terrace, followed by his lieutenant. Javier is a trafficker with Colombia's longest-surviving drug cartel, the Envigado Office, but he describes his work in matter-of-fact terms.

"The Office controls the illegal businesses in Medellín. Its main businesses are extortion, hired killings, the traffic in arms and drugs," he says.

The heavy security is soon explained: Javier fears his cartel—and his home city—may be on the brink of another drug war.

Colombia was supposed to have overcome its bloody history. Over the last decade, the government has pushed leftist rebels back into jungles, overseen the demobilisation of tens of thousands of illegal far-right militia fighters and taken down various drug *capos.*

Toby Muse, "New Drug Gang Wars Blow Colombian City's Revival Apart," *Guardian* online, April 10, 2012. www.theguardian.com. Copyright © 2012 Guardian News and Media Limited. All rights reserved. Reproduced by permission.

Washington foreign policy mandarins such as Paul Wolfowitz have held up Colombia as a model for other countries struggling with narco-chaos, such as Afghanistan and Mexico.

And Medellín, Colombia's industrial heartland, was promoted as the embodiment of the country's renaissance: the murder rate plummeted by about 80% over five years, reaching a decade low of 34 deaths per 100,000 in 2007. Once called the "city of death," Medellín was now open for business.

Medellín's homicide rate doubled in 2009, leaving about 3,000 people dead.

Cocaine and Gangs

But the root cause of Colombia's violence—the country's status as the world's biggest cocaine producer—has not disappeared. And Medellín's apparent peace lasted only as long as its underworld was run by one man, through the Envigado Office.

Named after a neighbourhood of Medellín, the Office was originally a group of hitmen acting for Pablo Escobar's cartel. After Escobar's death in 1993, the Office was taken over by a former ally turned bitter rival of Escobar, Diego Murillo, known as Don Berna, who cemented control over Medellín and moved the organisation deeper into drug-trafficking.

The Office will collect on anyone's debt, as long as the creditor is willing to give over 50% of what is recovered. It has its own motto: "Debts get paid—with money or with life."

"Many people know that the government won't act as it should, it won't help the people in what they need. Many people come to us to collect money, debts on cars, debts for drugs, basically anything," says Javier.

In his book *The Multinational of Crime: The Terrifying Office of Envigado*, journalist Alfredo Serrano writes: "Whenever anyone died, people would say that 'they had got on the wrong side of the Office'—as if this criminal organisation held the power of life itself."

Murillo handed himself in to the authorities in 2005 as part of a peace process with the far-right paramilitary groups, but was accused of continuing to run the Office from behind bars, which eventually led to his extradition to the United States. He was convicted of exporting tonnes of cocaine and sentenced to 31 years in an American prison.

After his conviction, the then head of the US Drug Enforcement Administration said: "American and Colombian communities are safer with the removal of this notorious drug kingpin."

But it would not prove so for Medellín. With Murillo out of the way, a vicious power struggle erupted between his successors. Medellín's homicide rate doubled in 2009, leaving about 3,000 people dead.

"Around 15 close friends were killed in the war. We couldn't go out to clubs, we just had to stay home and not get killed," says Javier.

The factional fighting within the Office came to an end last year with the capture of one of the rival leaders, and since then most of the group has reunited under a new boss, just in time to confront a new threat: one of Colombia's emerging narco-militias, the Urabeños.

Struggle for Power

The Urabeños sprang up after the peace deal with the far-right paramilitaries. While the main militia leaders were jailed alongside Don Berna, most of the mid-range commanders—those who had been running the day-to-day cocaine operations—were free. Many of these commanders reorganised their old outfits, recruited other demobilised fighters, and returned to drug-running.

The Urabeños are now a force across much of northern Colombia, bringing a military discipline to organised crime.

"They don't think like average narcos," said Jeremy McDermott, founder of Insight Crime, a thinktank that tracks organised crime in Latin America. "They are extraordinarily political, mixed with deep criminal experience."

The group's power was felt earlier this year when it forced dozens of towns to close all businesses after authorities killed an Urbaño leader. And now they are eyeing Medellín.

The looming battle between the Office and the Urbaños is for control of Medellín's underworld, the vast local market and for positioning to be able to negotiate with the Mexican mafias that ship cocaine to the US.

Cracking down on the Office will not be enough to keep the peace in Medellín.

"Many Colombians are moving over to Mexico to firm up relations," says Javier. "We get our guns from there and they get the drugs from us."

Earlier this month, a city-wide police sweep targeted gangs including the Office, arresting 49 people, including seven due for extradition. Last month, the brother of the current leader of the Office was arrested.

But observers say cracking down on the Office will not be enough to keep the peace in Medellín. Jesús Sánchez, who heads the human rights office for the city's ombudsman, says the local government must offer legal alternatives to the legions of hitmen who would fight any drug war.

"The state must do more than just attack the crime; the state needs a greater presence in the poor neighbourhoods," he said.

Infrastructure in the slums has improved, but Sánchez says the city still owes its young men a historical debt: two generations have grown up in a culture of violence and the easy money of trafficking. "When a young man doesn't find work, he's got the chance immediately to join a gang and get all the money he needs."

Javier doesn't see Medellín emerging from its problems soon. "If this is going to change, people must really want to change. But people always want money and power."

Gangster Trials Highlight China's Crime Battle

Sky Canaves

Sky Canaves is a writer and editor for the Wall Street Journal.

A series of criminal trials in Chongqing, one of China's biggest cities, is spotlighting a byproduct of the country's rapid social and economic change: the spread of organized crime.

Underworld Empire

The court in Chongqing, a city of more than 30 million people, is expected to reach verdicts in coming weeks on the charges against two prominent defendants.

Wen Qiang, the former head of Chongqing's municipal justice department, is charged with using his official position to provide protection to organized-crime gangs. Li Qiang, a billionaire businessman who was until recently a member of the local legislature, faces nine charges, including organizing and leading criminal gangs, bribery and tax evasion.

Officials say the two men ran an underworld empire that included prostitution rings, illegal casinos, bribery and murder.

The Chongqing crackdown is the largest local operation against organized crime in 60 years of Communist Party rule, according to Wang Li, a law professor at Southwest University in Chongqing. Some 800 people have been formally arrested and more than 2,000 others detained. A dozen high-ranking officials and hundreds of civil servants have been implicated.

The trials have focused national attention on a scourge that has mushroomed since China began economic reforms in the late 1970s. The situation has worsened over the past decade, as rapid development—combined with loosening controls on individuals, limited law-enforcement resources and widespread corruption—has created an environment in which gangsters thrive, often in collusion with local authorities, say experts.

While experts say gang activity doesn't appear to have infiltrated the highest levels of China's government, it is an increasing challenge for China's Communist Party, which rates public anger about corruption as a major potential threat to its rule.

In Chongqing, Bo Xilai, a former commerce minister installed as the city's chief in 2007, has turned up the heat on the issue. "The mafia crackdown is emphatically demanded by the people, as revealed to us by the numerous blood-shedding crimes," he is quoted as saying by the central Communist Party Web site.

In addition to infiltrating Chongqing's government, organized crime has moved into sectors from property development to privately run bus routes to pork products.

The government says police have broken up nearly 13,000 gangs and detained 870,000 suspects since the latest nationwide crackdown began in early 2006. Some 89,000 of those had been formally arrested as of September [2009], according to the state-run Xinhua news agency.

"Organized crime in China is coming back with a vengeance," says Ko-lin Chin, a criminologist at Rutgers University who studies Chinese gangs.

In addition to infiltrating Chongqing's government, organized crime has moved into sectors from property development to privately run bus routes to pork products, officials say.

Mr. Wen's sister-in-law, known as "the Godmother of Chongqing," has already been sentenced to 18 years in prison and fined around one million yuan ($146,000) after her conviction on charges including organizing and leading a criminal group, operating illegal casinos, illegal imprisonment and bribing officials. A pair of 23-year-old twins received sentences of 17 years apiece on convictions of organizing and leading a criminal group and intentional injury of others, among other charges.

Judicial and law-enforcement officials in Chongqing have declined to comment on the cases.

Since the Chongqing trials began in October, dozens of gang members elsewhere in China have also been sentenced, with at least 18 receiving death penalties.

In early December, a court in the southwestern city of Kunming sentenced five people to death for involvement in a gang that dealt in drugs, counterfeit money, fraud and racketeering. In southern China, a court in Yangjiang sentenced five men, including mob bosses nicknamed "Hammerhead" and "Spicy Qin," to death for murder and for running a massive illegal gambling empire. In Sichuan, police arrested 85 people in what officials called the largest drug bust in China's history.

At times, ties between gangsters and governments have eroded public trust, sometimes pushing individuals to take matters into their own hands.

Government and Gangsters

Organized crime was rampant in China before the communists took over in 1949, but was largely extinguished in the decades afterward by the totalitarian Maoist state [led by Communist leader Mao Tse-Tung]. It has flourished since reforms began in the late 1970s.

Chinese police receive small salaries but enjoy almost unchecked power over the increasingly wealthy communities they oversee. As a result, bribery is common, experts say. Without protection from law enforcement, "criminal organizations would not be able to develop on such a large scale and to such a high level," says Pu Yongjian, a professor at the business school of Chongqing University.

In some cases, police are discouraged by local governments from cracking down on prostitution, gambling and loan-sharking, as long as violence isn't involved, says Mr. Chin of Rutgers.

"These are very profitable businesses," he says. "They support the local economies and are seen as part of a transition period towards development. There is a boundary—kind of an implicit understanding—between local officials and mafia-like gangs."

At times, ties between gangsters and governments have eroded public trust, sometimes pushing individuals to take matters into their own hands.

In September 2008, 18-year-old Zhang Xuping, of Xiashuixi village in Shanxi province, stabbed the local party chief to death. Villagers allege the official ran a gang that used harassment and violence to take over their farmland. Mr. Zhang's mother, Wang Hou'e, had previously spent a year in detention after she complained to authorities about property damage she attributed to the party boss.

Officials in the district government that administers Xiashuixi declined to comment.

"I wish that we would have as aggressive a crackdown in our area as there is in Chongqing," says Ms. Wang. "My true feeling is that the mafia forces will not only continue to exist, but become even more rampant."

Central American *Maras*: From Youth Street Gangs to Transnational Protection Rackets

José Miguel Cruz

José Miguel Cruz is a visiting associate professor in the department of politics and international relations at Florida International University. He has been the director of the University Institute of Public Opinion at the University of Central America in San Salvador and worked as a consultant for the World Bank, the Inter-American Development Bank, and the United Nations Development Program on the topic of Central American violence. He is the author of Street Gangs in Central America.

There has been important discussion in the literature as to whether street gangs develop into organised crime groups. The recent development of turf-based youth gangs into powerful crime syndicates in Central America, South Africa, Brazil, and the United States seems to endorse the view that street gangs may evolve into complex criminal groups in different contexts. Hence, the most important questions regarding the research on gangs are not whether they can evolve into more sophisticated crime groups, but, rather, why and how some youth street gangs end up as racketeering networks, sometimes with transnational links.

Strengthening Gangs

From very different perspectives, contemporary authors, such as John Hagedorn and John Sullivan, have focused their attention on the processes of gang strengthening across time. Hage-

José Miguel Cruz, "Central American *Maras*: From Youth Street Gangs to Transnational Protection Rackets," *Global Crime*, vol. 11, no. 4, November 20, 2010, pp. 379–387.

dorn, on the one hand, stressed the role of local conditions, such as prisons, urban spaces, drug markets, and ethnic identities, in the persistence and growth of some gangs, a process he calls 'gang institutionalization'. On the other hand, Sullivan pointed to the contribution of communication technologies in the evolution of gangs. Both authors saw institutionalisation and evolution of gangs as related to globalisation; but whereas Hagedorn saw gangs reacting to socioeconomic transformations prompted by globalisation, Sullivan conceived gangs as taking advantage of the information revolution to wage 'netwar'.

Central American gangs have varied widely throughout the years; their formation into a network with features of protection rackets is part of a dynamic process.

In examining how Central American gangs, locally known as *maras*, evolved from youth street gangs to transnational groups with apparent features of protection racket gangs, I highlight the interaction between local conditions (marginalisation and law enforcement strategies) and transnational processes (migration and diffusion of Southern California gang identities). Instead of talking about globalisation, which may be a very broad and nebulous concept, I concentrate on the role of migration as a mechanism of exchange of norms and identities that facilitate the constitution of transnational networks. I argue that more important than the role of communication technologies, we have to examine the interplay between transnational norms and identities, and local factors. Street gangs in Central America used those assets provided by migration to survive and cope with local conditions. In the process, they ended up strengthened and transformed into loose networks with the capacity of ruling regional protection rackets. . . .

Central American *Maras*, Street Gangs, and Organised Crime

To understand the evolution of Central American *maras*, three definitions are in order: street gangs, organised crime, and *maras*. First, when referring to a street gang, I will follow [M.W.] Klein and [C.L.] Maxson's proposed definition, namely, 'any durable, street oriented youth group whose involvement in illegal activity is part of its group identity'. This concept is broad enough to accommodate all the fundamental characteristics—durability, street-oriented, youth, illegal activity, and collective identity—of the groups inhabiting any contemporary city and who used to dwell in El Salvador, Honduras, and Guatemala during the 1980s and 1990s. Second, instead of following the definitions of organised crime that have populated the gang literature thus far, and which have concentrated in the entrepreneurial and organisational features of some drug-trafficking American gangs, I will stick to Charles Tilly's notion that 'protection rackets represent organized crime at its smoothest'. In this sense, organised crime would be understood as any group with the capability to develop an illegal system in which the members of the group demand money from someone to provide protection against any threat or to avoid any harm perpetrated by the same members of the group. This notion also draws from the works of Thomas Schelling and Diego Gambetta who stress the monopolistic nature of the activity and put the threat of violence as key means in the economic activity of the gang. Finally, I will conceptualise Central American *maras* as a vast network of groups of people associated with the identity franchises of two street gangs that had their origins in the city of Los Angeles in the United States, but whose development no longer depends upon the American dynamics: the Mara Salvatrucha Thirteen (MS-13) and the Eighteenth Street Gang (also known as Barrio 18). These gangs, who now dwell in northern Central America, make up two separate transnational networks that have undergone a clear process of institutionalisation throughout the last few years that, in some places, is enabling them to become organised protection rackets.

According to some estimates, by the late 2000s there were approximately 67,000 *mara* members in Central America, with 36,000 living in Honduras, 17,000 in El Salvador, and 14,000 in Guatemala. These groups also have thousands of members living in the United States, particularly in Southern California and the Washington, D.C. area, where the Central American migrants concentrate. Research institutions and law enforcement agencies agree that these gangs are responsible for a substantial share of the criminal violence in Guatemala, El Salvador, and Honduras. For example, police figures indicate that around 55% of the nearly 1600 homicides committed in El Salvador between January and June 2008 were related to street gangs. In Guatemala, *maras* carried out 14% of the 5885 murders committed during 2006; and in Honduras, authorities maintain that gangs are responsible for 45% of the homicides. Although these figures must be taken cautiously, every observer of the Central American violence agrees that gangs are important actors of violence in the region. As maintained by an USAID report, *maras* conduct international business including the trafficking of illegal substances, kidnapping, robbery, assassinations, and other illicit profit generating activities. But the most distinctive feature of contemporary *maras* is their formation of protection racket rings whose leaders operate from prisons. According to the director of the Salvadoran National Civilian Police, 70% of the extortions committed in El Salvador are carried out by *maras*. Gangs extort money from local convenience stores, transport unions, and informal vendors at the streets. An investigation conducted by the Guatemalan police in a suburban town of Guatemala City revealed that *maras* collect nearly 4 million dollars every year from 'taxes' imposed on small business and transport unions that operate in the communities. A survey conducted by

Demoscopia in a sample of poor neighbourhoods in El Salvador, Guatemala, and Honduras showed that around 20% of small business pay 'protection taxes' to *maras*; in addition, in Guatemala, 28% of residents of poor communities have to pay taxes to gangs; 34% in El Salvador; and 31% in Honduras. Furthermore, according to former gang members interviewed in the same study, a single Salvadoran gang member weekly collects around US$1250, whereas a Guatemalan gang member collects US$975, and a Honduran gang member makes US$935 every week.

> *Migration flows between Central America and the United States bridged different gang phenomena that originally appeared and developed separately.*

Central American gangs have varied widely throughout the years; their formation into a network with features of protection rackets is part of a dynamic process and this article is also an attempt to capture the stages through which gangs expanded, formalised, and transnationalised, underscoring the variables contributing to this process according to local empirical research. Here, I argue that although marginalisation is important to understand the emergence of street gangs in Southern California and Central America, migration across the region and law enforcement policies in Guatemala, El Salvador, and Honduras are more important to comprehend their rise as loose transnational networks and powerful local protection rackets.

Migration and the Transnational Networking of Gangs

Many authors place the origins of the Central American gangs as a direct outcome of the migration of Central Americans, especially from El Salvador, since the early 1980s. The phenomenon is far more complex than that. Migration has definitely played a fundamental role in the expansion and development of the Central American gang problem, but it is important to point out that this factor does not explain how they really started. Gangs appeared in Central American countries long before refugees began returning following the Central American civil wars and before American immigration policies led to the deportation of numerous gang members back to El Salvador, Guatemala, and Honduras. In fact, the first studies in Guatemala and El Salvador on Central American gangs, already called *maras* by this point, appeared before the impact of migration began to be reported. These studies show that even though street gangs were already considered to be causing a serious problem with violence in some of the region's cities, none of the early hypotheses blamed the impact of migration or the deportation of young people from the United States.

When the political strife concluded in Central America in the early 1990s, immigrants in the United States, mostly Salvadorans, began making their way back home while the US government started a policy of mass deportations.

However, migration did contribute to the reconfiguration of gangs by facilitating the flow of identities, norms, and symbols associated with gang membership. . . . Migration flows between Central America and the United States bridged different gang phenomena that originally appeared and developed separately.

How did this process take place? Central America in the early 1980s was plagued with civil wars and military conflicts. This political instability pushed many Central Americans, especially Salvadorans, to emigrate, first as political refugees to the United States and later as economic refugees. Thousands of young Salvadoran immigrants grew up in Californian streets, especially in Los Angeles. There they associated with other Latin Americans, mostly Chicano and Mexican immigrants, who had formed their own gangs long ago.

Living in a cultural and economic disadvantage and often neglected by their parents in a particularly hostile environment, many young migrants found identity and peer support in the gangs. First, they joined Mexican and Chicano gangs; one of those gangs was the Eighteenth Street Gang. Later, as an outcome of the growing Salvadoran population, they began to form a separate gang with their own identity; this is the context in which the Mara Salvatrucha gang began, made up primarily of young Salvadoran immigrants, who were later joined by people from other Central American countries.

Meanwhile, in Central America, particularly in Guatemala and El Salvador, the conditions created by social exclusion, galloping urbanisation, the socio-political disarray caused by military conflicts, and problematic family dynamics led to the emergence of street gangs. This phenomenon, however, was characterised by the presence of a large number of different gangs that controlled specific, well-defined neighbourhoods and streets in the city. During the 1980s, street gangs in Guatemala and El Salvador were small groups of youth whose collective identities were, in many cases, determined by the turf they controlled. For example, in Guatemala, some of the gangs called themselves *Los Sacaojos, Los Capitol, Los Five*, etc. In El Salvador, gangs were even more fragmented, that is, there was a wider range of groups: *Mara Morazán, Mara Gallo, Mara Quiñónez, Mara AC/DC, Mara No-se-dice*, Mau-Mau, etc.

Displaced Young Men

When the political strife concluded in Central America in the early 1990s, immigrants in the United States, mostly Salvadorans, began making their way back home while the US government started a policy of mass deportations. In the 14 months after the peace treaty, over 375,000 Salvadorans voluntarily returned from the United States. In addition, more than 150,000 Central Americans were forced to return to their home countries in a 3-year period during the mid-1990s. These processes generated an influx of young people; some of them were bringing gang experience and a particular culture of being gang members. Most of the returnees were young males who had grown up in a completely different culture. They barely spoke Spanish, had weak family ties in the country of their birth, and, in some cases, had no reference group because their family and friends remained in the United States. The following statement from a Salvadoran young male who joined an existing gang in El Salvador after being deported illustrates such feelings:

> 'We're family. We're always there. When I first came here, the next day I met the homies. I saw the opportunity they gave us, because being there is like being in the gang. Nothing changes. We are from nine different gangs here (in this focus group), we're from different cliques, and most of us don't have any family left here (in El Salvador); and even if we had family here, they wouldn't support us.'

He meant that many of their first and most significant contacts with Central American society took place through the local gangs. These contacts facilitated, at first, the transmission of the symbols for being a gang member: their dress code, the use of tattoos, and means of communication, which resembled the Hispanic gang profile in Southern California. But more importantly, they transmitted American gang identities and, with them, a sense of belonging to gangs that have been originated in the United States.

One of the first manifestations of this reworking process can be found in the expression used in Guatemala for *maras* that got their names from the gangs of Los Angeles—*mara clones*—called this way 'because they are copies of similar foreign groups, the product of the impact of outside cultures, primarily from the United States'. By the early 1990s, one could find the Mara Salvatrucha and the Eighteenth Street Gang among the existing variety of gangs in San Salvador and White Fence and Latin Kings among Guatemalan groups. However, this situation did not last long. Influenced by the growing influx of returnees and the aura of admiration surrounding young people who had returned from California, the majority of the existing gangs in El Salvador and Guatemala first, and in Honduras later, began to adopt the ways and aesthetics of returning gang members—deportees or not. Over a span of 5 years, the gang identities from the United States spread out throughout the region, not through violence or turf wars, but rather through straightforward imitation and the gradual adaptation of identities.

Local gang members ... began at first to imitate the styles of the returnees and later ended up changing the names of their groups to one of the two gangs most accessible of the US model—Mara Salvatrucha (MS-13) or the Eighteenth Street Gang.

Two Honduran gang members interviewed as part of the research project *Maras y pandillas en Centroamérica* illustrate this point:

'The first *mara* I belonged to was the Latin Kings. It was formed by two dudes who came from the U.S.A. One from Los Angeles the other from Miami. They were all tattooed (. . .). They had an awesome Van, always riding a pretty chick in there. I saw them and dreamt being like them, because they looked gutsy and nobody messed with them.' (Honduran MS-13 gang member).

'The dudes who started MS-13 here were Lana and Toby. They came using huge trousers. . . . They always had a gun in their pockets but you wouldn't notice. We always learned from them . . . since they were coming from the U.S.' (Honduran Eighteenth Street Gang member).

Turf Gangs to Cliques

Local gang members, already active and organised into their own groups, began at first to imitate the styles of the returnees and later ended up changing the names of their groups to one of the two gangs most accessible of the US model—Mara Salvatrucha (MS-13) or the Eighteenth Street Gang. As part of this process, small gang groups formed clusters that shared the same name and then gradually adopted a system of behaviour, norms, and values that made them part of the same organisation. In this way, the old turf gangs turned into cliques—called *clikas* in Spanish—that made up a federation of gangs recognised as a single *barrio*—either Eighteenth Street Gang or MS-13. These cliques were turf-based as each of them controlled a specific neighbourhood, with relative independence from the rest of cliques.

However, the young returnees responsible for importing the US Hispanic gang culture model played an important role not only in the process of transplanting youth identities, but also in the process of configuring these federations into informal local-city networks. They were the ones who established contacts among the different groups that made up the gang, which permitted the flow of information and norms from abroad, and also among the local cliques. They acted as informal gang brokers in the Central American countries.

By 1996, according to a survey conducted with active gang members in the San Salvador Metropolitan Area (SSMA), 85% of young people in gangs belonged to the Mara Salvatrucha or the Eighteenth Street Gang; only 15% of gang members belonged to other gangs. A similar survey conducted in Honduras showed that MS-13 and the Eighteenth Street Gang controlled 85% of the gang members in Tegucigalpa and San Pedro Sula. However, in terms of numbers, the share of gang members repatriated from the United States was rather low. The survey in San Salvador revealed that 17% of active gang members in the SSMA had been in the United States and that only 11% had belonged to gangs while in the United States. The vast majority of *mara* members had joined in different Salvadoran cities. On a subsequent survey conducted in 2001, data showed that the percentage of gang members in San Salvador who have joined in the United States had increased only to 12%.

This process repeated itself in more or less the same fashion in Guatemala and Honduras, which were also impacted by the migration of their citizens to the United States. Just as in El Salvador, by the late 1990s, both Guatemala and Honduras had moved towards the model of two large gang confederations, although some small native gang groups persisted.

Although it is impossible to understand the formation of Central American *maras* as networks with disregard for the migration flows between the United States and Central American countries, it is important to acknowledge that the proliferation of youth gangs in Central America had already started before the bulk of returning migration took place. As Maxson and colleagues have pointed out in the case of American street gangs, local factors have larger influence in the formation and expansion of local cliques than migration. In the end, two phenomena that arose in relative independence and with their own dynamics of causality ended up coming together and forming part of a single regional system of networks that now covers northern Central America and several American cities.

In Russia, Anti-Drug Gangs Hunt Down "Spice" Dealers

Mansur Mirovalev

Mansur Mirovalev reports on Russia for the Associated Press.

Two men in their early twenties lie face down in the snow, hands tied behind their backs, heads doused with dark red paint. A dozen young men, some wearing surgical masks, wreck a car with hammers and axes. One sets fire to a plastic bag filled with a greenish powder and a stack of cards that read: "Aroma, Smoking mixes."

A New Drug

The powder is a synthetic drug known as "spice" that is Russia's latest scourge. The pair on the ground are alleged pushers. And the hammer-wielding men? Vigilantes fighting the drug's spread with widespread public approval, admiring television coverage—and, according to critics, the Kremlin's tacit blessing.

The anti-drug gangs roaming streets in Moscow and other urban centers are an offshoot of the pro-Kremlin youth movement Young Russia. The vigilantes, who call themselves the Young Anti-Drugs Special Forces, have tapped into rising public outrage over the spread of drug use in Russia, and the impotence of law enforcement to stop it. They are also stirring concerns about President Vladimir Putin's perceived tolerance for extralegal actions against forces considered harmful to the regime or to public order.

Young Russia and a half dozen other pro-Kremlin youth groups were formed in the mid-2000s, analysts and opposition figures say, to prevent street protests similar to those that ushered pro-Western opposition forces into power in three ex-Soviet states: Georgia, Ukraine and Kyrgyzstan. Russian authorities are accused of encouraging violence, or the threat of violence, by youth gangs when dealing with what they see as threats to stability. The vigilantes' free hand indicates that the spice epidemic is seen as one of [these] threats.

The Interior Ministry, which controls Russia's police, declined comment to The Associated Press on the gangs, which suspended their activities this month without explanation. The head of Russia's anti-drugs agency, Viktor Ivanov, criticized the group's actions as illegal and "nothing but noise."

Spice consists of herbs coated in chemicals that mimic the effects of marijuana, cocaine and methamphetamine. In recent years, millions here, mostly teenagers, have smoked various kinds of spice, attracted by its cheapness, availability and reputation for being harmless, officials and anti-drug campaigners say. Reliable figures on usage are not available because of the variety of kinds of spice on offer and the lack of official studies on the phenomenon.

Fighting spice is nearly impossible, because banning one or more ingredients means manufacturers simply change the molecular structure of the chemicals or replace the herbs to skirt the law.

Pushers sell bags of spice for less than $15, in schools or online, from bulletproof cars and shops with barred windows and metal doors. Their phone numbers are often scrawled on walls or sidewalks, or printed on business cards that carry messages such as "100 percent harmless smoking mix" and "Smoke and go to paradise." Some pushers never see their customers and text message the whereabouts of a spice stash after getting a money transfer.

Spice is mass produced in China and Southeast Asia and exported to Russia as bath salts, incense and slimming additives, often in mail packages.

Ivanov, who heads Russia's Federal Drug Control Agency, said fighting spice is nearly impossible, because banning one or more ingredients means manufacturers simply change the molecular structure of the chemicals or replace the herbs to skirt the law.

"There are 900 versions of it, and every week they come up with a new one," Ivanov told The Associated Press.

Masked Men

And that's where the masked men with hammers come in. The Anti-Drugs Special Forces, widely known by their Russian acronym, MAS, was formed last year and includes dozens of activists in Moscow, many of them with a background in martial arts. Leaders say the group gets funding from donors and small city-run construction projects that its volunteers work on.

And the group has its own formula for hunting down spice traders. They track down a pusher. One of them uses a hidden camera to videotape a "control purchase." And then a dozen or more attack, while one or two of them shoot video.

They sometimes face no resistance from lone pushers who beg to be released and swear never to sell spice anymore. Other times, they fail to break into their fortified shops, leaving after painting the doors and bullet-proof windows with graffiti saying: "Drugs are sold here" or "They kill your children with impunity." On rare occasions, pushers fight back or call their bosses—burly men with guns and knives.

An Associated Press reporter observed the Moscow attacks on the two pushers who were doused with red paint in the snow.

Screaming obscenities and threats, more than a dozen vigilantes wearing masks and holding hammers surrounded a man with a baseball bat who had just jumped out of a parked car. The man moved backward, swinging his bat as several masked vigilantes closed in. The driver sat in the car, face convulsed with fear.

The attackers broke a window of the car and threw in a smoke candle, forcing the driver out. They punched and kicked him, tied his arms and legs with duct-tape and threw him to the snow, dousing his head with paint. From the car's front seat, they took a plastic bag with spice and set it afire. Seconds later, the first man was tied up and also soaked in paint. The assailants smashed the car with metal bars and hammers and turned it on its side.

[One vigilante] group claims to have conducted more than 300 raids over the past year in Moscow alone, and posts many raid videos online.

The group admits that its methods are illegal.

"We're walking on the edge, but you have to understand that fighting drugs is a serious thing," said group leader Alexei Grunichev, fair-haired and gaunt, while showing raid videos on his laptop at the group's headquarters in several decrepit rooms. "We also understand our guilt for what we do, but I think that what we do is right and we will fight, keep fighting using these methods until law enforcement agencies, authorities can put everything under control."

Hardcore Solutions

The group claims to have conducted more than 300 raids over the past year in Moscow alone, and posts many raid videos online. These short clips are the backbone of the group's reputation and popular support—despite the violence, obscenities and property damage they contain. They are available on YouTube, the website of their mother group, Young Russia, and on the group's page on vk.com, Russia's most popular social networking site.

MAF issued a low-key statement on vk.com this month saying that it had halted drug raids on April 12 [2013]. However, the group's main website does not mention the suspension and still advertises its hardcore solutions to the spice use problem.

Hundreds of Russians leave encouraging messages on the group's webpages, young rappers praise them in songs and Russian television networks run reports on the group's raids.

"People often say, 'You should just kill those pushers,' although that's not the way we work," says Arkady Grichishkin, an agitated 21-year-old martial arts student often seen on the group's videos as a leader of raids.

The Federal Drugs Control Agency said it does not condone the group's raids.

"We cannot welcome it," said Ivanov. "It lies beyond law—first of all. And secondly, it makes nothing but noise." The vigilantes, however, appear to see Ivanov as an ally, posting his portrait on the walls of their headquarters.

Users say that the high they get is extremely intense and hallucinogenic. After several weeks of using spice, the drug causes sleep and weight loss, hypertension, seizures and can even lead to schizophrenia, according to officials, health experts and studies in Russia, EU and the U.S.

Users' parents also appear to be worried.

"Eighty per cent of phone calls our hot line gets are about spice," says Alexander Bysov of the Moscow-based Sodeistvie—or Assistance—anti-drugs fund that has a hotline for drug addicts and their parents and runs a rehab. "Parents are already crying SOS."

Gangs of Rio

Mac Margolis

Mac Margolis is a Bloomberg View *contributor based in Rio de Janeiro. He has reported on Latin America for* Newsweek *and has been a frequent contributor to* The Economist, The Washington Post, *and* Foreign Policy. *He is the author of* The Last New World: The Conquest of the Amazon Frontier.

Gardênia Azul, a flatland slum in the scruffy west end of Rio de Janeiro, isn't much to look at. But don't tell that to Juliana. She moved there from Cidade de Deus (City of God), the bullet-riddled shantytown featured in the eponymous drugs-and-thugs film of 2002 that rattled polite Brazilians and earned Latin America's fairest address lasting notoriety. At least in Gardênia there were no teenagers with Kalashnikovs or vendors hawking cocaine in the street. To Juliana, a manicurist with a four-year-old son, those things matter. "We can walk the streets any time of day or night," she says, "I feel safe."

Private Enforcers

In Gardênia Azul safety is relative, and comes at a price. It's the six percent markup that residents pay on a bottled gas for cooking or the steep rents the slumlords charge. Or the fact that Juliana prefers not to use her real name when talking to a reporter. The reason for her reticence is "the militia," a self-designated neighborhood police force that runs the favela with an iron heel and a hand in everyone's pocket, taking a cut of all local business and services. No one is fond of the militia, which is often the corrupt twin of legitimate law enforcement with rogue cops acting as judge, jury and occasionally executioner. (Juliana won't soon forget her neighbor's 16-year-old, who was shot dead for smoking marijuana, his body dumped in the main square.) But to millions of people trying to get by in some of the meanest streets in the hemisphere, life involves hedging your bets by grabbing at whatever safety net you can. Cariocas, as city natives are called, light one candle to Cristo Redentor, the Art Deco Christ watching over Rio from the mountains, and another to the *caveirão*, the armored car police use to raid the outlaw favelas. And since neither authority has been up to the task, now the Cariocas are turning to the market.

Lately the market is booming. Blackwater gets all the press for its controversial work providing private security in Iraq, but more and more cities around the world have surrendered crime fighting and prevention into private hands. Analysts estimate that policing is a $100 billion to $200 billion global business and a growth industry in the developing world. In Russia, private cops outnumber regular ones by 10 to 1. So ubiquitous are they in South Africa, militias are even tasked with guarding regular police stations. Private security generates an estimated million jobs a year in India. Even Uganda has 20,000 private police on the streets, as many as Iraq had in 2006, at the height of the war.

Militia bosses have parlayed their lock on the favelas . . . into personal fortunes, including yachts, mansions, and country estates.

Driving the trend is a complex demographic upheaval of rising prosperity in the emerging nations, a widening gap between rich and poor, burgeoning slums, and the utter incapacity of official enforcers to keep pace with outlaws. In the world's more orderly cities, where there are shopping malls to keep safe, upstanding companies like Pinkerton or the U.K. based G4S deploy trained and uniformed guards and work closely with official law enforcers. The reality is far different in the poorest countries, where the superrich are tailed by heavies in black suits and earpieces while the poor are left to fend for themselves. The contrast is especially stark in Rio, where some 800 shantytowns crowd the glistening skyline or fester around shuttered factories. For decades, drug traffickers held a monopoly in these asphalt no-man's lands. Now the militias have staked their claim.

Worse, Rio's militias are not just tolerated but exploited by crooked officials, who parlay their official status into a lucrative franchise. Many militias are composed of off duty cops, cashiered prison guards, firefighters, and even condemned criminals who take orders from senior police and elected officials. A recent probe by Rio lawmakers named eight elected officials and 67 police as ringleaders in 171 favelas. Don't bother asking for badge numbers. "You've heard of the gangs of New York. Now we have the gangs of Rio," says Claudio Ferraz, who heads Rio's organized-crime fighting [unit], DRACO.

Crime and Politics

These official godfathers are what makes militias far more treacherous than drug traffickers, says José Mariano Beltrame, Rio's secretary of public safety. "We are seeing the criminalization of politics and the politicization of crime," he says. And yet Beltrame says before he took office in 2007 no one even bothered to investigate the militias. Why the blind spot? "Interests," he shakes his head, signaling he can say no more. A probe by the Rio daily *O Dia* found that militia bosses have parlayed their lock on the favelas—where they run public transportation, skim off utility payments, control home sales and rentals, and peddle pirate cable-TV subscriptions—into personal fortunes, including yachts, mansions, and country estates.

The good news is the official indulgence may be ending. A former chief of police is now behind bars, for allegedly commanding militias. And after raiding militia strongholds and arresting more than 60 alleged ringleaders in Campo Grande, a major suburb west of Rio, the murder rate there plunged, a flicker of hope for the rest of the city. Still, busting rogue cops is only the beginning. Last month, a notorious militiaman known to all as Batman and serving time for attempted murder, walked out of a maximum-security prison in broad daylight. "Criminals move in where the state is weak or absent," says state lawmaker Marcelo Freixo. He should know. The target of anonymous threats ever since he led the legislative probe into Rio's militias, Freixo never goes anywhere without the cloud of body guards he refers to as "my friends." In Rio, everyone hedges their bets.

Indonesia Field Report I—Crime as a Mirror of Politics: Urban Gangs in Indonesia

Vanda Felbab-Brown

Vanda Felbab-Brown is a senior fellow with the Center for 21st Century Security and Intelligence in the foreign policy program at the Brookings Institution. She is an expert on international and internal conflicts and nontraditional security threats, including insurgency, organized crime, urban violence, and illicit economies.

There are many types of gangs in Indonesia and they vary in their savviness of how to accumulate power, cultivate political connections, and acquire political capital. Rather surprisingly, many Indonesian gangs frequently do not appear to provide extensive socio-economic services to the communities where they operate or deliver otherwise absent public goods, beyond providing protection and security. Many of the street vendors I interviewed throughout Java and in Sumatra, for example, complained about the gang taxes and claimed that the gangs were of little use to them and appeared to welcome when the state acted to suppress the gangs.

Many Different Gangs

Some are informal organizations of soldiers and sailors out for fun after dark, and one would not expect them to have political ambitions or organize services parallel to or in the absence of the state. Neither would one expect such behavior from the motorcycle gangs, such as the Moonraker, Grab on Road (GBR), and Exalt to Coitus (XTC), that operate in Indonesia. But since Indonesia moves on mopeds and motorcycles, distinguishing a motorcycle gang of the Hells Angels-type from a gang that employs the typical Asian means of transportation may be tricky.

Indeed, the labeling of groups and individuals as *preman* (with the term encompassing everything from a criminal, street tough, to an outright organized crime group) has often been used and misused for political purposes. As much as the formal state institutions and political parties have used the gangs for their purposes, they have also often found it convenient to make the gangs and, more broadly, the urban poor their scapegoats. Many underprivileged urban young, or homeless people and beggars have been labeled *preman* merely because they are poor and live in a slum. Similarly, the Indonesian police have a tendency to call even peaceable groups of young kids just hanging around on the streets *preman*.

One of the most powerful gangs and most visibly used as a tool of the political order and highest formal political power is Pemuda Pancasilla.

Some gangs, such as ... John Kei's Key Youth Force, are ethnically based. The *transmigrasi* policy[1] encouraged population movements throughout the archipelago—mostly Javanese and southern Sulawesi natives moving to other islands; and, inevitably, quite apart from the *transmigrasi* policy, Jakarta's economic growth and opportunities attracted migrants from elsewhere. With poor skills and lacking access to established patronage networks, they would often languish in Jakarta's slums, with particular ethnic groups settling down in particu-

---

1. A policy of moving people from populated regions to less populated parts of Indonesia. It began in the late nineteenth century and continues today.

lar areas. The young unemployed become easy recruiting targets for ethnically-based gangs. The wider ethnic-minority community would depend on the gang for access to formal and informal jobs and other patronage, with other ethnic enclaves and their gangs remaining closed to outsiders. Some of the prominent ethnically-based gangs have included groups from Ambon, the Moluccas, Timor, and southern Sulawesi, particularly Makassar.

Gangs and Politics

Violence between the ethnically-based gangs has occasionally not only triggered violent confrontations in the criminal market, but also set off wider ethnic violence in Indonesia. The November 1998 Ketapang riot in West Jakarta between gangs from Ambon and Flores, provoked by clashes over the control of parking lots and a gambling den, was believed to be the last spark igniting the ethnic and sectarian violence in Ambon during the late 1990s and early 2000s. But that narrative may have merely provided a convenient excuse for the police and military forces to be supporting Betawi (Jakarta native) gangs since then. Of course, ethnic tensions over access to land and state resources in Ambon had been growing for a number of years and were intensified by the [radical] Islamist salafi global mobilization of the 1990s. (The ethnic violence itself, despite its terrible human toll, provided Indonesia's military and law enforcement forces with a plausible justification to keep high budgets after the collapse of the Suharto regime [in 1998].)

But the gangs that do provide socio-economic services and hobnob with the politicians can accumulate a great deal of political power. Indeed, it is often very difficult to draw clear distinctions between some gangs and formal political youth organizations in Indonesia. The two entities may strongly overlap in leadership and membership, with each being unique and separate only at the margins. The gangs with the most explicit and thickest connections to formal political parties pro-vide—rather naturally—the most extensive socio-economic and social services beyond protection, such as street cleaning, electricity, water distribution and sewage, flood assistance, and blood donations. They also resolve disputes, whether over land in slum areas without formal justice institutions and rule of law, or even among businessmen who choose to risk going through Indonesia's corrupt and increasingly unpredictably bribable courts. Importantly, they also deliver votes for their political sponsors, put on mass rallies to demonstrate the par-ticular political party's street power, intimidate opponents, and break up the opponents' rallies or labor strikes. Both the gangs and youth organizations help local party bosses to win public goods tenders and are themselves rewarded with such tenders by their political overlords.

One of the most powerful gangs and most visibly used as a tool of the political order and highest formal political power is Pemuda Pancasilla [PP]. A criminal gang with large mem-bership on the one hand, it also managed to present itself as the ultimate defender of Indonesian nationalism and the New Order of [longtime dictator] President Suharto. Established in the early 1980s in Sumatra, it grew under the leadership of Yapto Soerjosoemarno to claim a pan-ethnic membership of 10 million throughout the archipelago in the late 1990s. Often doing the bidding of Indonesia's military and intelligence ser-vices or Suharto's political party (Golkar) it coerced support for Suharto's regime, beat up opponents and extorted the Chi-nese business community for private rents and political dona-tions, as well as partook in charitable activities and the provi-sion of socio-economic goods to local communities. It also provided privileged access to jobs. Unlike the gangs that the Indonesian state employed after the creation of Indonesia and those that had been used by Indonesian political actors even during the colonial, pre-independence days, PP succeeded in sufficiently covering its origins and connections to the criminal underworld so as to portray itself as the ultimate voice and carrier of the official ideology and values of the Suharto's regime.

After Suharto

Given how tight with the Suharto regime PP was, it is not surprising that it did not weather well the end of the Suharto regime. After the end of Suharto's reign, Pemuda Pancasilla tried to transform itself into an official political party, and twice, under different names, it did very poorly in national elections. It still exists as a youth group and a street gang, but it now needs to share power in the criminal market and in the political space far more than ever before with other gangs-cum-political-organizations.

The selective embrace of some of the preman *and targeted repression of other gangs is nothing new in Indonesia.*

The criminal gangs that emerged in the wake of the collapse of the Suharto regime have reflected the diversification of political cleavages in Indonesia. Many have remained ethnically-based. Not surprisingly, some of [the] most successful urban gangs have been those that have received the most support from the post-Suharto state and law enforcement—namely, Jakarta's Betawi gangs, such as the Betawi Brotherhood Forum (FBR) and the Betawi People's Forum (Forkabi), based on ethnic groups "native" to Jakarta. By supporting them, the security services believe they have a better capacity to control outbreaks of ethnic violence beyond the criminal market. By the late 2000s, the Betawi groups displaced other ethnically-based groups from large areas of Jakarta, such as Tanah Abang area.

Reflecting the new era of Indonesia's Islamization during the 2000 decade, the Betawi gangs have also embraced Islamist narratives. Donning Islamic regalia, they have at times taken it upon themselves to enforce sharia [Islamic religious law] and harass the Christian and Ahmadyyia minorities in West Java— both because of genuine ideological drive and because such actions would make them politically useful to politicians mobilizing on the basis of Islamization as well as generate various resources, including access to land, and other economic rents for the gangs. This coating with Islam too made them appealing to Indonesia's military and law enforcement agencies, which since the early 1990s have also become increasingly Islamized.

Picking Favorite Gangs

The selective embrace of some of the *preman* and targeted repression of other gangs is nothing new in Indonesia. The most brutal campaign of such selective weeding out of the gangs who were most troubling for the regime and cooptation of those most useful to the regime took place in the early 1980s. Suharto's so-called *Petrus* campaign (short for mysterious killings) viciously and rather indiscriminately targeted all manner of "inconvenients"—unemployed youth, disobedient criminal gangs, or those supporting Suharto's rival General Ali Moertopo, and sometimes even just street children. At the end of the campaign, between 5,000 and 10,000 people were killed.

Although far less violent than during the Suharto era, the anti-preman repression waves during the 2000 decade have continued to target political criminal enemies as well as to cater to the growing middle-class fears of criminality and distract the broader body politic from other problems, such as the country's socio-economic difficulties, and also away from having to fundamentally redesign the tight relationship between the state and political parties and criminals. Like the *mano dura* policies in El Salvador and Central America, the suppression campaigns would target vulnerable marginalized individuals merely because they sported a tattoo, and would flood the jails with low-level offenders or members of targeted criminals simply on the basis of their membership, rather than any evidence of actual criminal behavior. But this seemingly indiscriminate repression has consciously coincided with highly-selected nurturing of some cultivated "friendly" gangs.

A policy of incomplete, selective repression is ... much cheaper than addressing the basic socio-economic and public safety deficiencies that trouble Indonesia's sprawling slums.

Indonesia's politicians continue to be deeply complicit in the perpetuation of the state-crime/cooptation-repression pattern, for fundamentally breaking with the system would require their sacrificing the various advantages they get from employing the criminal gangs. It is far easier and more convenient to occasionally give in to periodic public outrcries for anti-crime campaigns and to round up the most vulnerable people.

In labeling the sponsorship of favorite proxies and ethnic-kin vigilantism as "community policing," politicians and law enforcement agencies in Indonesia put a new face over the past decade on old practices. Often underwritten with a lot of money, such "community" initiatives and "community partners" would receive official blessing to cleanse areas, such as Tanah Abang in Jakarta, of ethnic and business rivals. At the same time, in a classic Mansur Olson fashion, the repression waves have made membership in a gang all the more valuable: those without membership and sponsorship would be more vulnerable to arrest and have more difficulties obtaining patronage. Within certain bounds, gang membership would materially, politically, and psychologically empower marginalized individuals, while, paradoxically, by reinforcing the pressures toward gang membership within the slums, gang leaders and politicians as well as police and military officials would profit from the repressive anti-gang campaings.

Getting Away with Murder

Such a policy of incomplete, selective repression is also much cheaper than addressing the basic socio-economic and public safety deficiencies that trouble Indonesia's sprawling slums. Rather than bringing the state into the slum in a comprehensive, multifaceted, and accountable manner, periodic selective repression allows the powers that be to get away with murder (literally and figuratively) while minimizing the resources necessary to suppress crime and manipulate it for one's purposes. In the long term, the outcome is a profound marginalization of vast segments of society and perpetuation of political and socio-economic conditions that give rise to alienation and that sever bonds between citizens and the state, but in the short term, such an approach is cheap and delivers benefits to adroit politicians and law enforcement agents.

Organizations to Contact

The editors have compiled the following list of organizations concerned with the issues debated in this book. The descriptions are derived from materials provided by the organizations. All have publications or information available for interested readers. The list was compiled on the date of publication of the present volume; names, addresses, phone and fax numbers, and e-mail and Internet addresses may change. Be aware that many organizations take several weeks or longer to respond to inquiries, so allow as much time as possible.

American Civil Liberties Union (ACLU)
125 Broad St., 18th Floor, New York, NY   10004-2400
(888) 567-2258
e-mail: aclu@aclu.org
website: www.aclu.org

Founded in 1920, the American Civil Liberties Union (ACLU) is a national organization that works to defend civil liberties in the United States. It publishes various materials on the Bill of Rights, including regular in-depth reports, the newsletter *Civil Liberties*, and a set of handbooks on individual rights. The organization often opposes anti-gang legislation on civil liberties grounds.

Bureau of Justice Statistics (BJS)
United States Department of Justice
810 Seventh St. NW, Washington, DC   20531
(202) 307-0765
e-mail: askbjs@usdoj.gov
website: www.ojp.usdoj.gov/bjs

The mission of the US Department of Justice's Bureau of Justice Statistics (BJS) is to collect, analyze, publish, and disseminate information on crime, criminal offenders, victims of crime, and the operation of justice systems at all levels of government. These data are critical to federal, state, and local policy makers in combating crime and ensuring that justice is both efficient and evenhanded, BJS's website offers a clearinghouse of statistics from all areas of criminal justice, including gangs and gang prevention.

Cato Institute

1000 Massachusetts Ave. NW, Washington, DC 20001
(202) 842-0200 • fax: (202) 842-3490
e-mail: cato@cato.org
website: www.cato.org

The Cato Institute is a libertarian public policy research foundation. It evaluates government policies and offers reform proposals in its publication *Policy Analysis*. In addition, the Institute publishes the bimonthly newsletter *Cato Policy Report* and the triannual *Cato Journal*. It works against gun control legislation and against drug war policies and mass incarceration.

Drug Enforcement Administration (DEA)

Mailstop: AXS, 2401 Jefferson Davis Hwy.
Alexandria, VA 22301
(202) 307-1000
website: www.dea.gov

The Drug Enforcement Administration (DEA) is the federal agency charged with enforcing the nation's drug laws. The organization concentrates on stopping the smuggling and distribution of narcotics in the United States and abroad. It publishes *Microgram Journal* biannually, *Microgram Bulletin* monthly, and drug prevention booklets, such as *Get It Straight* and *Speaking Out Against Drug Legalization*.

National Crime Prevention Council (NCPC)

2345 Crystal Dr., Suite 500, Arlington, VA 22202
(202) 466-6272 • fax: (202) 296-1356
website: www.ncpc.org

The National Crime Prevention Council (NCPC) provides training and technical assistance to groups and individuals interested in crime prevention. It advocates job training and recreation programs as a means to reduce crime and violence. Its website includes news and press releases and information on crime safety, including discussions of gang prevention and drug and alcohol abuse.

National Criminal Justice Reference Service (NCJRS)

US Department of Justice, PO Box 6000
Rockville, MD   20849-6000
(800) 851-3420
website: www.ncjrs.gov

The National Criminal Justice Reference Service (NCJRS) is one of the most extensive sources of information on criminal justice in the world. The agency's website provides topical searches and reading lists on many areas of criminal justice. Numerous publications on juveniles, the justice system, drugs, crime, and other topics are available at its website. NCJRS also publishes a National Youth Gang Survey and various reports, such as "Getting Out of Gangs, Staying Out of Gangs."

National Urban League

120 Wall St., New York, NY   10005
(212) 558-5600 • fax: (212) 344-5332
website: www.nul.org

A community service agency, the National Urban League aims to eliminate institutional racism in the United States. It also provides services for minorities who experience discrimination in employment, housing, welfare, and other areas. Its website includes news reports and publications such as *Opportunity Journal*, *Urban Influence Magazine*, and others.

Organized Crime and Gang Section (OCGS)

US Department of Justice, Criminal Division, OCGS
1301 New York Ave. NW, Washington, DC   20005

(202) 514-3594
website: www.justice.gov/criminal/ocgs

The US Department of Justice Criminal Division's Organized Crime and Gang Section (OCGS) is a specialized group of prosecutors charged with developing and implementing strategies to disrupt and dismantle the most significant regional, national, and international gangs and organized crime groups. It assists with the federal investigation and prosecution of organized crime cases. Its website includes information about organized crime and gangs as well as news and press releases.

RAND Corporation

1700 Main St., PO Box 2138, Santa Monica, CA   90407-2138
(310) 393-0411 • fax: (310) 393-4818
website: www.rand.org

The RAND Corporation is a research institution that seeks to improve public policy through research and analysis. RAND's Drug Policy Research Center disseminates information on the costs, prevention, and treatment of alcohol and drug abuse as well as on trends in drug-law enforcement. Its extensive list of publications includes "Crime Entry and Exit Among Brazilian Youth" and many white papers and reports on US drug policy.

V2K H.E.L.P.E.R. Foundation

610 California Ave., Venice, CA   90291
(310) 823-6100
e-mail: help@helperfoundation.org
website: http://helperfoundation.org

The V2K H.E.L.P.E.R. Foundation, formerly known as Venice 2000, is a nonprofit that works to prevent gangs and gang violence through community intervention. It has been involved in negotiating peace agreements between rival gangs and also engages in counseling, leadership training, mentoring, job development, and youth workshops. Its website includes information on its programs and services.

Bibliography

Books

Radley Balko   *Rise of the Warrior Cop: The Militarization of America's Police Force.* New York: PublicAffairs, 2013.

Randol Contreras   *The Stickup Kids: Race, Drugs, Violence, and the American Dream.* Berkeley: University of California Press, 2012.

Robert J. Duran   *Gang Life in Two Cities: An Insider's Journey.* New York: Columbia University Press, 2013.

Edward Orozco   *God's Gangs: Barrio Ministry,*
Flores   *Masculinity, and Gang Recovery.* New York: NYU Press, 2013.

Ioan Grillo   *El Narco: Inside Mexico's Criminal Insurgency.* London: Bloomsbury Press, 2011.

James C. Howell   *Gangs in America's Communities.* Thousand Oaks, CA: Sage Publications, 2012.

Malcolm W. Klein   *Street Gang Patterns and Policies.* New
and Cheryl L.   York: Oxford University Press, 2006.
Maxson

John R. Lott Jr.   *More Guns, Less Crime: Understanding Crime and Gun Control Laws,* 3rd ed. Chicago: University of Chicago Press, 2010.

Jeff Pearce — *Gangs in Canada*. Auburn, WA: Lone Pine Publishing, 2010.

Victor M. Rios — *Punished: Policing the Lives of Black and Latino Boys*. New York: NYU Press, 2011.

Reymundo Sanchez and Sonia Rodriguez — *Lady Q: The Rise and Fall of a Latin Queen*. Chicago: Chicago Review Press, 2008.

Irving A. Spergel — *Reducing Youth Gang Violence: The Little Village Gang Project in Chicago*. Lanham, MD: Altamira Press, 2013.

Frederic Milton Thrasher — *The Gang: A Study of 1,313 Gangs in Chicago*. Chicago: University of Chicago Press, 2013.

Sudhir Venkatesh — *Gang Leader for a Day: A Rogue Sociologist Takes to the Streets*. New York: Penguin Books, 2008.

Daniel W. Webster and Jon S. Vernick, eds. — *Reducing Gun Violence in America*. Baltimore, MD: Johns Hopkins University Press, 2013.

Periodicals and Internet Sources

BBC News — "Mexico Mayor 'Killed for Standing Up to Drugs Cartel,'" November 8, 2013. www.bbc.co.uk.

Robert Beckhusen — "As Colombian Drug Gangs Collapse, Mexican Cartels Get Tons of Cheap Coke," *Wired*, April 11, 2013. www.wired.com.

Matthew Blake   "The New Face of Chicago Gang Violence," *Progress Illinois*, September 24, 2012. www.progressillinois.com.

Maggie Caldwell and Josh Harkinson   "50 Days Without Food: The California Prison Hunger Strike Explained," *Mother Jones*, August 27, 2013.

Christian Science Monitor   "After Chicago Shooting of Girl, a Fresh Look at Gang Gun Violence," January 31, 2013.

Ta-Nehisi Coates   "The Social Trends Driving American Gangs and Gun Violence," *Atlantic*, February 14, 2013.

Charles C.W. Cooke   "Chicago, Guns, and Obama," *National Review Online*, February 11, 2013. www.nationalreview.com.

Mike Dumke   "How Stop and Frisk Works in Chicago," *Chicago Reader*, August 26, 2013. www.chicagoreader.com.

Ed Grabianowski   "How Street Gangs Work," HowStuffWorks, 2007. www.howstuffworks.com.

Meghan Grant and Kyle Bakx   "Nick Chan and the Decline of Calgary's Notorious FOB Gang," CBC News, August 27, 2013. www.cbc.ca.

Johann Hari   "The Only Thing Drug Gangs and Cartels Fear Is Legalization," *Huffington Post*, August 26, 2010. www.huffingtonpost.com.

Melissa Howell   "Will Targeting Gangs in Burlington
                        Lead to Racial Profiling?,"
                        WCAX.com, July 24, 2013.

Kevin Johnson   "Cities Across the USA Fight to
                        Control Street Gangs," *USA Today*,
                        June 4, 2012.

Trymaine Lee   "Gun Violence and Murder Are on
                        the Decline in Chicago," MSNBC,
                        November 28, 2013.
                        www.msnbc.com.

John Lippert   "Heroin Pushed on Chicago by
                        Cartel Fueling Gang Murders,"
                        Bloomberg, September 16, 2013.
                        www.bloomberg.com.

Mary Mitchell   "Civil Rights Leaders Should Get
                        Involved in Gang Summit," *Chicago
                        Sun-Times*, September 23, 2013.

New York Times   "More Disclosures About
                        Stop-and-Frisk," November 29, 2013.

University of   "A Brief Outline of Chicago's Gang
Illinois at Chicago   History," n.d. www.uic.edu.

Alexa Vaughn   "Seattle Gang Tensions, Violence on
                        Rise," *Seattle Times*, May 30, 2013.

Sudhi Venkatesh   "Understanding Kids, Gangs, and
                        Guns," *New York Times*, October 3,
                        2012.

Index

H

I

J

K